CREATIVE VISUALIZATION

How to use Imagery and Imagination for Self-Improvement.

CREATIVE VISUALIZATION

by

Ronald Shone

THORSONS PUBLISHERS LIMITED
Wellingborough · New York

Published in the U.K. by Thorsons Publishers Ltd., Denington Estate,
Wellingborough, Northants NN8 2RQ and in the USA by
Thorsons Publishers Inc., 377 Park Avenue South, New York 10016.
Thorsons Publishers Inc. are distributed to the trade by
Inner Traditions International Limited, New York.

First published 1984
Second Impression 1985

British Library Cataloguing in Publication Data

Shone, Ronald
  Creative visualization.
  1. Creative thinking
  I. Title
  153.3'5   BF408

  ISBN 0-7225-0830-1

Printed and bound in Great Britain

CONTENTS

INTRODUCTION

Many of the new developments in expanded consciousness have realized the importance of imagery and the use of creative visualization. This return of interest, however, is fairly new and is scattered throughout different psychologies. But they all utilize creative visualization in the same way. The obvious realization is that people have *learned not to use their imaginations* and consequently this facility has diminished. Imagery, however, is a natural feature of the nervous system and it can soon be re-learnt.

This book is concerned with a discussion of imagery and in particular creative visualization. In Part I we deal with some conceptual issues. Because imagery has largely been ignored in standard courses on psychology we begin by discussing this and how it is the basis of imagination. Even in this chapter we supply ideas on how to improve imagery and imagination. In Chapter 2 we discuss dreams. The reason for this is to show that dreams utilize creative visualization quite naturally and we can learn from these when consciously creating images. A person's behaviour is very much dominated by their self-image: in Chapter 3 we discuss some speculative views about 'Self' and how this knowledge can aid in calling on 'inner guides'. This chapter tries to draw on Eastern ideas and apply them in a way that appeals to the West. In the final chapter in Part I we draw together many of the principles and propositions which are contained throughout the book.

Part II is more practical. It illustrates how to *develop* and *use* creative visualization in everyday situations. The aim has been to choose situations found in all aspects of living. We begin in Chapter 5 with imagery in business situations because most of us spend many hours at work. This is followed by ideas of using creative visualization in your leisure hours. Here we concentrate on sport, although the ideas can be used in the same way for hobbies in general. In Chapter 7 we turn to a very common problem, shyness, which is often tolerated but nothing usually done about it. This illustrates how creative visualization can be used for changing behaviour. In the next chapter we discuss how creative visualization is used in the improvement of memory; memory is so important, yet often ignored as if nothing can be done to improve it. Chapter 9 uses creative visualization to achieve goals. Here we concentrate on the importance of creative visualization in achieving success. Chapter 10 shows how creative visualization can help in relieving pain and improving health. In the final chapter a general creative visualization is given for raising your energy level, with some brief comments on other uses.

Although the range of topics is quite wide you will soon realize that they all basically follow the same format; it then becomes much easier to form images and utilize creative visualization in virtually any aspect of living.

One final comment on the structure of the book: Part II occasionally refers to Part I, but it is possible to read Part II before or after Part I. You may like to read both parts concurrently, depending on your interest. Chapter 4, listing the principles and propositions, along with their location, will help here. This chapter acts like a summary of the book.

Two aspects, however, run through the whole book. First, the importance of the two hemispheres of the brain and how creative visualization largely calls on right brain features. Second, all exercises are done while in a relaxed state. The next two sections deal with each of these aspects respectively.

Right and Left Hemispheres of the Brain
Creative visualization is carried out in the brain: it is in the brain where we create images. But we must learn (re-learn?)

how to do this efficiently. One of the most important observations to have come out of recent work on the brain is that the two hemispheres of the brain function in different ways. For instance, language is usually a function of the left hemisphere while spacial orientation is a function of the right hemisphere (where we shall refer to the hemispheres as the left brain and the right brain). The most usual division of functions between the right and left hemispheres is shown in Figure 1. It is clear from this figure that the left brain is the logical reasoning brain while the right brain is used for functions which require objects and behaviour to be assessed as a whole (i.e. holistically).

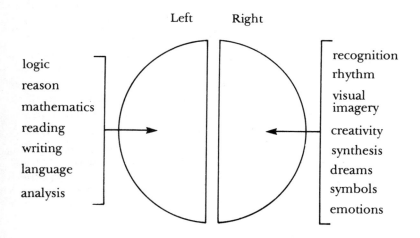

Left Right

logic
reason
mathematics
reading
writing
language
analysis

recognition
rhythm
visual
imagery
creativity
synthesis
dreams
symbols
emotions

Figure 1

Suppose I asked you to calculate the sum of one-half of ten and one-third of nine. You would use the left brain to do this calculation. If, however, I asked you to recall a beach on your last holiday, you would utilize the features of the right brain. Images, which we deal with in detail in the first chapter, are a feature of the right brain. Dreams, which we shall deal with in detail in Chapter 2, are also a feature of the right brain. *Creative visualization is a feature of the right brain.* The scientist is largely left brain dominated while the artist is largely right brain dominated. Leonardo da Vinci and Einstein almost certainly had both brains functioning in balance and utilized them in co-operation. For the most effective use of creative visualization it is important that the functions of the right hemisphere of the brain are improved. Many of the exercises in this book will, in fact, help to do this.

The State of Relaxation for Engaging in All Exercises

All the exercises in this book are to be undertaken while in a relaxed state. This may be achieved either by means of self hypnosis, as outlined in my *Autohypnosis*, or by any method of your own choosing. However the state is attained, you should achieve the situation where your eyes are closed. your breathing is slow and regular and your muscles are relaxed. You can be either lying down or sitting in a chair. If sitting, then you should have your back straight, your feet flat on the floor and your arms in a comfortable position. Here I shall outline a simple progressive relaxation routine which you can use for the exercises throughout this book.

First get into a lying position or sit straight in a chair, close your eyes and begin breathing slowly and regularly. Then repeat the following suggestions to yourself and as you do so concentrate your mind (your consciousness) on the part of the body being referred to. For instance, when you say 'relax the left foot', concentrate your mind on your left foot. And so on up the body.

State of relaxation

My feet are very relaxed; my left foot is very relaxed. My left ankle is relaxed and as my left foot relaxes, so I am becoming more and more relaxed. And now my left calf muscle is becoming very relaxed, very relaxed indeed. And the relaxation is spreading up my left leg and into my left thigh. And now the whole of my left leg is very relaxed indeed. (Now do the same with the right leg.)

And now the relaxation is spreading up my body. My pelvis is very relaxed and all the muscles of my stomach are very relaxed, yes very relaxed indeed. And I am feeling warm, relaxed and comfortable. It is as though there is a sun in the pit of my stomach radiating warm glows which are spreading throughout my body. And now my chest muscles are relaxing, very, very relaxed. All my body is very relaxed.

My shoulder muscles are now relaxing. Very, very relaxed, just as all the other muscles have relaxed and are going to continue to relax. And now the muscles of my left arm are relaxing. They are becoming very limp and relaxed. All the muscles in my left arm are becoming very limp and relaxed. And now my left hand is also becoming very relaxed, just like the remainder of my body. (Now do the same for the right arm and right hand.)

Now the muscles of my neck are relaxing. Yes, they are becoming very relaxed indeed. All tension is going from my neck and the muscles are becoming very limp and relaxed. Yes, all the muscles in the back of the neck are becoming very relaxed indeed. And now the muscles of my face, my ears and around my eyes are relaxing. The muscles of my brow are relaxing. Yes, all the muscles of my face and head are becoming very relaxed, just like the rest of my body.

Although this series of suggestions takes a long time to describe, it does not take very long to perform. Furthermore, in time you can achieve the relaxed state very quickly indeed, and so can dispense with this. It is, however, therapeutic in its own right, and so if you wish simply to relax and build up your energy level you can engage in this along with the suggestions given in the final chapter.

PART I

1
IMAGERY AND IMAGINATION

As the title of this book indicates, we are very much concerned with using the imagination to visualize things; not simply to reproduce them in memory, but creatively to visualize them. In this chapter the intention is to discuss some of the more formal aspects of imagery and imagination. This is necessary because the dominance of behavioural psychology has meant that very little work has been done on these topics. Behaviourism, with its emphasis on the objectively observable and testable, banned subjective analysis from psychology. Images and the use of the imagination *are* subjective experiences and so they were not discussed – attention instead was directed at the behaviour of rats, birds and other animals which could be experimentally tested. We, therefore, begin our discussion with an overview of this methodological debate. In the next section we consider in detail the type of images which can be formed. Although this book is largely concerned with visual images, other images are available and can be used in just the same way. Having discussed images we turn, in the next section, to that of the imagination – in particular, a discussion of what it is. This, too, is important because throughout this book we shall make a distinction between 'imagination' and 'creative imagination'. Having established that we all can create images and so have an imagination, we next turn to how it is possible to develop these. In the final section we take up the connection between the imagination and the will. Although the will is even less precise, and even more subjective, than the imagination, the relationship between them is important because it is generally misunderstood – being a remnant from a Victorian idea of willpower.

Like all the chapters in Part I, the points being raised are largely theoretical in nature. The practical aspects of imagery and the creative use of the imagination will be developed more fully in Part II.

The Neglect of Imagery and the Imagination

Behaviourism began in the early 1900s and dominated psychology for many years. In essence, behaviourism asserts that the only thing that can be studied by psychologists is what can be *observed*. Subjective experiences cannot be tested and therefore, they argue, should not be discussed. This was a natural outgrowth of 'logical positivism' which also concerned itself with testable (i.e. refutable) hypotheses. Logical positivists would argue that any discussion about 'the existence of God' is not a meaningful question and, therefore, is not for discussion. In just the same way, behaviourists argued that an image formed by a person was particular to that person– it could not be observed, it could not be shared and nor could it be tested under experimental conditions. For behaviourists, therefore, it did not belong to the study of psychology. Dreams also are subjective and so they too were banned from study. Certainly, no behaviourist would contemplate even thinking about altered states of consciousness.

Behaviourism was a reaction against the earlier view of psychology which was dominated by introspection – and hence very subjective. But it went too far in its protestations (some would even say that it was the Dark Age of psychology). Like all swings of the pendulum, it is now returning. Behaviourism has much to offer (admittedly, more to offer about rats than about man!). The more recent development of cognitive psychology supplies a 'healthy' blend of the subjective and objective. With the rise of cognitive psychology, with its emphasis on learning and information processes, much has been learned about images formed by the mind. These researches are new and are related to work taking place in neurophysiology (see, for example, the very interesting discussion by M. Hunt in *The Universe Within*, 1982). This work will undoubtedly continue and will, hopefully, lead to a better understanding of imagery and the workings of the imagination.

Types of Images

Suppose I asked you, 'Where is your home?'. When answering such a question would you have an image in your mind of where your home is in relation to where you are now? Even if I simply said 'teapot'; would you simply remember the word? Would you picture a 'teapot' almost instinctively? If I asked you to describe in words what your mother looked like, would you simply remember or would you first create an image in your mind and then describe the image? Now think about 'church bells'. What is it that comes to mind? Finally, think about 'vinegar'. All these examples, to different degrees, combine both memory and images. The point is that we often remember by first creating an image.

Images are not only visual. We can have images of sound (auditory), of movement (kinesthetic or motor), of touch (tactile), etc. Undoubtedly, the most common image is visual. in terms of a sample of the population, the type of images and their percentage in ranking order are (McKellar, 1968):

Visual imagery	97
Auditory	93
Motor	74
Tactile	70
Gustatory	67
Olfactory	66
Pain	54
Temperature	43

This in itself is useful information. If you intend to improve your imagery, then you should concentrate on visual and auditory, since these are the easiest and will lead to the greatest success. This book concentrates on creative visualization and as such deals with visual imagery to a large extent. Given that most of the population have visual imagery then this emphasis is justified.

Why are visual images in the mind so important? The most important thing about visual images is that they can influence the body. This does not apply to all images, but only to those images in which *you* are involved. The image, however, does not have to be about reality, it can be a totally imaginary (unreal) image. In the mind's eye it is possible to place an image of oneself in a totally imaginary scene. But why go about this image formation? A strongly formed image will lead to an emotional response or some other bodily response. *It does not matter whether the image is about reality or something totally imaginary.* Both will create changes in the body which are consistent with the image. (Ask a small boy to imagine that he is brave and strong and you will see him straighten up and throw his chest out. In other words, the body is responding to the image being formed.)

But it is not only the body which is influenced by images. Behaviour, too, is influenced by them. Again the result is similar. *A strong image leads to behaviour consistent with the image being formed in the mind's eye.* It does not matter whether the image is one of reality or unreality. What matters is whether the image is *strong* and whether you have *belief* in the image.

What is generally lacking in image formation, especially when the image involves something which is not real, is an ability to create and hold a strong image. The reason for this is simply that we have not developed the skill. It has not been thought necessary to train a person in image formation. The fact that nearly everyone forms images and uses images as guides to their memory, does not mean that most people do it well. Everyone can speak (with a few exceptions) but some are better than others because they have practised it and been taught how to do it well. Creating images in the mind is no different. This type of training plays a central role in *psychosynthesis*, and a number of techniques for developing strong mental images can be found in Assagioli (1965) and Ferrucci (1982). Some of these we shall discuss in 'Developing the Imagination' on p.19.

What is Imagination?
Imagination is the mental faculty of forming images or concepts of external objects not present to the senses. Imagination, however, is very closely linked with daydreaming and fantasy. Daydreaming is the act of indulging in fancy or

reverie while awake; while fantasy is the faculty of inventing images. As pointed out earlier, behaviourism put an effective stop to research into subjective states of the mind – and imagination, daydreaming and fantasy are all subjective states. Fortunately, there has been a return of interest in such states, e.g. J. L. Singer's *Daydreaming and Fantasy*. In this section we shall not attempt to distinguish between these three faculties but concentrate on some tentative remarks about the imagination.

Although we cannot measure people's imaginative ability – at least not precisely – it is clear that people possess it. But research takes us no further. At our present state of knowledge we cannot answer the following questions:

- What is the imagination?
- What purpose does the imagination serve?
- How does the imagination function?
- Where is the imagination located?
- Has imagination changed over the course of history?
- What is the relationship between imagination and creativity?
- Is imagination positively or negatively related to language development?
- Who has a good imagination and why?
- Can the imagination be improved?
- Can a person have no imagination?

This list is by no means exhaustive, but it does highlight the extent of our ignorance about the imagination.

Given this ignorance, let me make a number of personal speculations about the imagination. First, imagery of some form, whether visual, auditory, or any one of the others listed in the previous section, would seem to be a basic element in our make-up. This would suggest that everyone has an imagination – the only difference is the degree. Second, the fact that visual images are the most frequent, and probably the most important, would suggest that imagination is an attribute of the nervous system which predates language. Language, however, has given imagination a new dimension which is almost as significant as the purely visual features of imagination. Third, the main groups to possess a good imagination are writers, artists, actors, poets, dancers and, above all, children.

The fact that children have a good imagination suggests that imagination is associated with those parts of the brain which are formed in the early years. Its poor state in later life would further suggest that it is simply neglected as language and other logical pursuits are concentrated on in the person's educational development. The fact that certain groups, such as poets and actors, retain and develop their imaginations as they grow older would suggest that it does not naturally diminish with age, but diminishes from lack of use (or by the design of the educational system). Fourth, image formation is a feature largely (although not wholly) of the right brain. This is supported by the points made in my third speculation on the imagination. Children are only beginning to develop their powers of reason; that is to say, they are only beginning to develop the faculties of their left brain. While this is going on, they can readily call on the faculty of imagination, with its dependence on imagery. Writers, artists, actors, poets, and dancers use many of the features of the right brain – imagery, synthesis, rhythm, etc. They have retained and developed their imaginations. Fifth, the age of reason has meant that all other faculties of the mind have been treated as less, or even of no, importance. Put bluntly: reason is more important than imagination! But this is placing reason and imagination in conflict with one another in such a way that a choice has to be made. However, reason and imagination are different things, each with their individual use and purpose. It is wrong to ask, Is reason more important than the imagination?'; the more appropriate question is, 'How can we develop both reason and the imagination?' Sixth, creativity is the ability to show imagination as well as routine skill. In other words, creativity is the *combining* of reason and the imagination. The creative person combines the features of the left brain with those of the right: reason with imagination.

Western dependence on reason has meant that we frown on such things as the imagination. Schooling develops reasoning powers and implicitly, if not explicitly, treats the imagination as unimportant. It is not surprising, therefore, that children very soon give up being imaginative. As this process continues the growing person finds it more and more difficult to form mental images, simply because this particular faculty goes unused. For such a person creative visualization is not easy. But remember, imagination is inherent in the nervous system and as such it can be relearned.

Developing the Imagination

From what has been argued in the previous section, it would appear that we all possess an imagination which most of us have simply left to diminish from lack of use. But how do we develop imagination? This can be done from two directions. First, by practising forming mental images. Second, by developing imaginative skills.

Developing mental images

Visual   Close your eyes and practise forming the following images in your mind's eye:

- numbers written on a board
- letters or words written on a board
- a coloured circle
- a coloured triangle
- a coloured square
- a crescent moon
- a star

If you have difficulty with any of these construct them on large sheets of white paper. Look at them for a few minutes and then visualize them in your mind's eye. This can be especially useful in the case of the coloured shapes. In the case of writing, visualize the page of a book with writing on. In the case of numbers see them on a page and begin to do addition and subtraction – visually.

Auditory   In your mind's eye recreate the following sounds. If you find them difficult, create a scene in which the sound is a natural part:

- a gong
- a voice calling your name
- children playing
- traffic
- a train
- a ship's horn
- a church bell

Kinesthetic (i.e. movement)　　In your mind's eye see, and most particularly feel, yourself doing the following:

- walking
- running
- swimming
- driving
- sawing wood
- dancing

Tactile　　In your mind's eye feel yourself doing the following:

- shaking hands
- stroking a cat (or dog)
- placing your hand in snow
- stroking a piece of wood
- placing your hand under running water
- running your fingers through soft wool

Gustatory　　In your mind's eye imagine what it's like to taste the following:

- your favourite dish
- an orange
- whipped cream
- ice-cream
- a hot drink
- a date (or fig)
- whisky (or some other spirit)

Olfactory　　In your mind's eye imagine what it's like to smell the following:

- perfume
- petrol
- freshly baked bread
- wood
- tar
- mint
- a rose

All these examples are purely illustrative and you can readily devise your own. The important point is to practise them. Since they are all done in the mind's eye then they can be practised anytime and anywhere – most especially when travelling. Nor are they independent of one another. When trying in your mind's eye to smell a rose, it is highly likely that you will also visualize one. Creating situations in which you are actively participating is a very good way to practise. This will also help in developing your imagination. For instance, imagine yourself, in your mind's eye, walking down the street. In the background you hear the church bells ringing out. In the street children are playing, you hear them clearly, and they are playing with a large red ball. A friendly dog comes up to you at this point, and you stroke it. And so on . . .

It is not just a question of remembering similar situations. The object is *to be in the scenes, seeing and feeling, smelling and tasting what you are creating*. It requires you to pay attention and concentrate on the images being created in your mind's eye. As you practise all these various images they become easier.

Developing imaginative skills
This is less straightforward. The object, however, is 'to be as a child'. If you present a child with a picture of a youngster with a guitar and then ask him or her to create a story to account for this, then you will observe the imagination in action. Some children with very vivid imaginations have imaginary companions (some go as far as to hallucinate these companions). As we get older we 'put away such childish things' but do not put anything in their place (with the possible exception of sexual fantasies). But there does appear to be a need to 'feed' the imagination, which most commonly arises in novels and films – most especially science fiction.

The simplest way to practise being imaginative is to *role-play*. Just as in the case of the child creating a story about the youngster with the guitar, you can be as imaginative as possible in fully creating the role and carrying it through in your mind's eye. Although you may feel a little foolish doing this for the first few times, there is no need because it is all done in the mind and no one need know you are doing it. If you give up readily it is a likely indication that you cannot carry it through, that you have a poor imagination. In this case you should increase the role-playing rather than decrease it.

To aid in developing your imaginative skill try the following role-playing:
- Hercules (or Aphrodite)
- Merlin the Magician
- Julius Caesar (or Cleopatra)

- a rabbit
- a sea gull
- a computer
- a £20 note

Such roles are the basis of fairy tales, mythology, novels and films. In literature, and more recently in scientific works comparing man and machines, you will find many imaginative essays written from an unusual vantage point – from Kafka's *Metamorphosis* to Harding's *On Having no Head*, this second reprinted in Hofstadter and Dennett (1981).

Imagination and the Will

The will is no match for a strong imagination. If the will and the imagination are in conflict then the imagination will win.

We have pointed out that little is known about the imagination, but even less is known about the will. It appears to be a force belonging to the inner self which gives direction and purpose to a number of things we do. For example, a blind boy may have 'the will to succeed at college against all odds'. The will acts as a means of marshalling the body's energies, emotions, drives, etc. into a purposeful and co-operative relationship. It has no obvious outward manifestation: it simply directs – like the conductor of an orchestra. Assagioli in *The Act of Will* puts it as follows:

> The most effective and satisfactory role of the will is not as a source of *direct* power or force, but as that function which, being at our command, can stimulate, regulate, and direct all the other functions and forces of our being so that they may lead us to our predetermined goal.

There is no intention here to discuss the will, suffice it to say that the will can direct the imagination in a purposeful way in order to achieve some stated goal. When an individual has no clear idea of the purpose of the will, then it is possible that the will and the imagination can be directed at two opposing purposes. When this happens, the person's behaviour is governed more by the imagination than by the will – this is especially true when the imagination is acting negatively. In Chapter 9 we shall discuss one method of bringing the will and the imagination into co-operation and not into conflict.

2
DREAMS AND SYMBOLS

Man has almost certainly dreamed from the very beginning, but dreams have defied scientific analysis. Even so, people persist in taking an interest in dreams and believe that they have a purpose (even if they do not know what it is) and that they have a meaning (no matter how bizarre they appear to be on the surface). Dreams are a personal subjective experience, and a particular dream is a one-off event which does not occur ever again (even recurring dreams are slightly different – only the basic content remains the same).

There are two quite distinct aspects to dreams:
(1)   the definition and description of dreaming,
(2)   the interpretation of dreams.
The definition and description of dreams involves the scientific study of dreams, which was only begun in the twentieth century. The interpretation of dreams has been a constant feature of man and recorded in mythology and in the bible. In the first two sections of this chapter we shall have a few remarks to make on the scientific study of dreams – if for no other purpose than to dispel some myths about dreams. In the final section we shall consider what we can learn from dreams as a help in developing creative visualization.

This chapter is not meant to be a study of dreams and their interpretation, a subject which could fill a number of books. Rather, the aim is to concentrate on those aspects of dreaming which give us some insight into how the right brain formulates and uses images. Once we distil this information we can use it *at the conscious level* as a means of carrying out creative visualization.

What Are Dreams?

The Penguin Dictionary of Psychology defines a dream in the following way:

> A train of hallucinatory experiences with a certain degree of coherence, but often confused and bizarre, taking place in the condition of sleep and similar conditions.

In simpler terms, dreams are images in the mind which are experienced during our hours of sleep. (Similar dream experiences can be undergone by means of drugs or hypnosis.) Because dreams occur when we are alseep, then it is clear that they are not generally part of our conscious mind, they belong to what we invariably call the unconscious or subconscious mind. When a dream is 'recalled' we mean that it is consciously remembered; i.e. it is brought into conscious awareness. When people say that they 'don't dream', what they in fact mean is that they do not, or cannot, bring their dreams into conscious awareness – that they cannot recall a dream. If a dream cannot be recalled then to all intents and purposes, the dream might as well not have taken place – it does not (consciously) exist. The difficulty is not in the dreaming but in the recall of dreams.

We now have our first clue as to why dreams often appear confused and bizarre. They appear only confused and bizarre to our conscious mind. And why is this? It is because our conscious mind is dominated by the left hemisphere of the brain. Our conscious mind, therefore, looks for logical patterns, linear associations, realistic patterns, etc. But dreams being a part of the subconscious mind are dominated by the right hemisphere of the brain and so are governed by other features – such as nonlinear patterns, emotional content, symbolism, etc. The patterns and associations created by the subconscious mind cannot readily be re-arranged into a logical pattern that the conscious mind can absorb. But then why should they?

It is like trying to study a fish out of water. You can see it wriggle and die. You can cut it up and observe its inside. But you can only appreciate a fish if you study it in its own environment. So, too, with a dream. You can study it at the conscious level, but you will not appreciate a dream outside its own environment – or better still, outside its own frame of reference. The common mistake in dream interpretation is in attempting to fit the dream into a frame of reference that appeals to the conscious mind. What needs to be done is to change the frame of reference. This, however, is easier said than done. Studies are only just beginning on how the right brain functions and processes information. It is this research which will supply us with the new frame of reference. All we can do at the present is realize that dreams operate on principles different from the conscious mind. They utilize features such as symbolism, nonlinear patterns, holism, time distortion and emotion.

One dream state is worthy of comment, and this is the *lucid dream*. A lucid dream is a state of dreaming where the person actually (i.e. consciously) knows that they are dreaming. It would appear, therefore, that a lucid dream occurs when some particular relationship exists between the conscious and subconscious mind (or the left and right brains). The nature of this relationship is not known. But like so many things we do not know, it is still possible (some argue) to bring about and increase lucid dreaming; see, for example, P. Garfield (1974, Chapter 6) and A. Faraday (1972 and 1974).

Facts, Myths and Symbolism

Intensive research into sleep and dreaming was undertaken when it was noticed that during certain periods of the sleep state the eyes rapidly moved under the eyelids. This became known as Rapid Eye Movement sleep (or REM sleep for short) or even paradoxical sleep. Later research found that during REM sleep a person was dreaming. So began a scientific study of sleep and dreaming.

It was soon discovered that everyone dreams during their period of sleep and that this takes place during REM sleep. This immediately disproved the myth that some people do not dream. What it demonstrates is that everyone dreams during sleep, but that dream recall can vary from zero (no recall) to almost 100 per cent (almost perfect recall). It also disproved the very common myth that dreams happen in a flash. Dreams take time and can occur over twenty minutes or more (usually during three REM periods in a night). In addition, certain foods, such as cheese, do not lead to more dreaming but, by disturbing sleep, increase the recall of dreams. A final myth that this research can dispel is the belief that dreams do not involve colour. Dreams do involve colour, but not in great quantities and the colour is soon forgotten.

We can obtain some insight into dreams and how they utilize the right brain, by considering what people actually dream about. One survey, undertaken by Calvin Hall and reported in *Scientific American*, indicates that people dream about dwelling places, conveyances (e.g. a car) and entire buildings. One usual interpretation for this predominance is that dreams reflect things going on in the subconscious mind, and that the subconscious is often represented in dreams by rooms in buildings. The majority of dreams have only a small number of characters – usually two in addition to the dreamer (although it is possible that all characters are simply different personalities of the self). Furthermore, the content of dreams reflect our emotional involvement with our family and friends. When considering behaviour most dreams involved movement (e.g. walking, running and riding); but not, contrary to popular opinion, falling or floating. Talking in dreams is quite common, and dreams generally involve passive or quiet activities rather than manual activities, although sporting and recreational activities are fairly frequent.

Dreams involve much emotional content, a particular feature of the right brain. The most frequent emotion felt was apprehension, with anger, happiness and excitement next. Although most dream content was negative or unpleasant, the dreamers themselves rated dreams as generally pleasant rather than unpleasant.

It would appear, then, that dreams are a form of thinking which occurs during sleep – a form of thinking which is characteristic of the right brain and not the left brain. The conceptions and ideas are not conveyed in words and logical reasoning, but rather in the form of images, most usually visual images (which is consistent with the information given in the previous chapter). The dreamer is concerned about him or herself: their fears and hopes, their anxieties and ambitions. When other people enter the dream it is only with respect to how they impinge on *his or her* existence. Because of this dreams are one of the most important sources of information we have about how people see themselves. They also reveal that people are dynamic and their conception of themselves changes constantly.

It has just been pointed out that dreams convey ideas and conceptions in the form of images. Because the information is conveyed usually in the form of pictures then symbols play an obviously important role in forming such pictures. Put another way, given dreams do not convey information in words and logical reasoning, then in what form can such information be conveyed? The symbolic meaning of dreams played a very important part in Freud's theory of dream interpretation and was extended in Jung's theory. These theories are too involved to go into here, but what is clear is that symbols play a very crucial role in dreams as a means of conveying information. When engaging in creative visualization, therefore, we should take note of this and use symbols in a very conscious way.

What Can We Learn From Dreams?
Dreams are not part of our conscious mind but rather of our unconscious. They indicate how the brain processes information in a way 'natural' to its internal workings; that is to say, when freed from the logical reasoning processes of the conscious mind, the unconscious mind processes information in a totally different way. There is no 'right' way to process information; it is a result of the development of the human nervous system – most particularly the brain. It is possible to argue that logical reasoning processes were devised as a means of living in the *external* world and relating to other people and things in the external world, while another form of processing information has been devised for *internal* workings of the individual.

What we learn from dreams is that pictures are very important in conveying information. Since dreams are largely (if not exclusively) about ourselves, then it would appear that we can best change our self-image by also using pictures. It is a two-way process. Dreams at any given moment of time give us a picture of our self-image. But the self-image can itself be influenced by means of creative visualization, as we shall indicate in the next chapter. This, in turn, will give rise to a different self-image in our dream. The important point is that you have more chance of changing your behaviour or the image of yourself by presenting to your mind (to your right brain, to your unconscious mind) a picture of how you would like to behave or like to be. It is, of course, possible to attempt to reason to yourself why you should change or why you should be a certain way, but this is not likely to bring about any change.

In a dream you are the central character, and often the only character. When engaging in creative visualization again you are the central character and it is quite easy to picture yourself in some setting or doing some activity. It is easy because you do it so frequently in your dreams. What matters when forming these pictures is the whole content of the picture, it is the whole which is conveying something to the mind.

In the same way, it is important to include emotion in creative visualization. Our dreams reveal our hopes, desires and anxieties. Emotion appeals to the right brain and gives involvement and commitment to what is contained in the picture. Hence, if you wish to change your behaviour or your self-image then it is important that you not only believe that the change is possible, but you must *want* it. The wanting is not wishful thinking, it is a means of incorporating emotion into the picture. *The emotion provides the energy for the transformation.* This should be borne in mind during all the exercises in Part II.

3
SELF-IMAGE AND
INNER GUIDES

In other parts of this book we will deal with more or less everyday things: pain, poor health, shyness, memory, success and sport. In this chapter I wish to explore some of the more speculative aspects of a person's psyche. I have labelled them 'inner guides', and sometimes they are referred to as inner gurus. A guru is a Hindu word for spiritual teacher – although it is now used in a much wider context to mean any spiritual teacher. In this chapter there is no intention to become involved in a discussion of religion. Rather, the aim is to give some comments on Eastern ideas which are gaining acceptance in the West. These ideas are not religious ideas as such, but they are connected with particular religions. What we wish to do is extract the idea from the religion. This is not difficult. Christ said, 'love thy neighbour as thyself'. If it was considered that this was a very sensible precept then one could accept it without embracing Christianity as such. Most important ideas are, for this reason, found in most religions around the world. It is the ideas which are important and not the organized religions in which they are usually embedded.

Since these ideas are not well documented in the West we shall take them slowly. We shall begin with a discussion of the term 'Self'. So far I have made a distinction between your 'outer self' and your 'true self'. What exactly is the difference? Are there other selves, such as the 'unconscious self' as distinct from the 'conscious self'? In the next section we discuss the idea that we are all a mixture of male and female, what in Tao (the philosophy of T'ai Chi) is referred to as the Yin and Yang. This introduces the idea that we have at least two inner guides, one male and one female – and most likely more than two. Having established the idea that we do contain such inner guides in our psyche, then we discuss the means of evoking them so that we may call on their help. In the final section we shall discuss what caution is necessary in interpreting these inner guides and carrying out what they say.

Various Meanings of 'Self'

This is a vast and complex topic and the intention here is to present some personal remarks about the meaning of 'Self' which may help the reader appreciate the importance and usefulness of calling upon 'inner guides'. The easiest way to appreciate the problem is to try to answer the question, 'What do I mean when I say "I"? For instance, if you say, 'I'm tired' or 'I feel hungry' or 'I want an ice-cream', are all these the same 'I's? In other words, is there a well defined *unchangeable* entity we call 'I'? You may remark that 'Of course there is!' But we readily distinguish between the conscious mind and the unconscious mind. Are these just two aspects of this one unchangeable 'I'? Furthermore, many of our wants are products of our personality. If these were developed as we grew up then can they be said to be part of our unchangeable 'I'?

These are very difficult questions to answer and they have been the concern of psychologists and philosophers throughout the world and throughout time. I shall present here my own view – and it is only a personal view.

A person is composed of many 'I's – if you like many persons. There is the child 'I' who likes or dislikes food, there is the sports 'I', and the shy 'I', the lovable 'I', and the decision-making 'I'. These and many others make up what we call personality – but what here is better thought of as many personalities (not simply 'the' personality). But there is also an inner 'I', a core of unchangeable 'I', what I have called your *true self* in other chapters. This true self can itself develop, it is not as if you are born with it ready formed. However, around it grows a 'false self', a set of personalities which are formed over the years as you grow older. These are determined by your environment, and most especially by the people you come into contact with. These false personalities make up both your conscious self and your unconscious self. Your conscious self, however, is only a small part of your existence.

Figure 2 may help clarify matters.

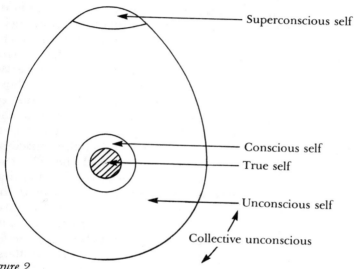

Figure 2

The outer ellipse is composed of the unconscious self. This has a greater sphere of influence than your conscious self, and so your conscious self can be thought of as a smaller sphere contained in the larger one. This sphere representing your conscious self is influenced by, and itself influences, your unconscious self. In the centre is your true self. By being in the centre and having the smallest sphere of influence, it indicates that both the conscious self and the unconscious self are influenced by it, but that because it is so small the conscious and unconscious selves have the greatest influence on behaviour at any moment of time. This representation can be elaborated to incorporate the higher self (or superconscious self) and collective unconscious. The superconscious self can be thought of as an area of the unconscious at the upper end, as shown in Figure 2, while the collective unconscious is the area outside the outer ellipse. For an elaboration of these views, see Assagioli (1965) and Ouspensky (1950, 1957).

The representation of the various selves that I have just outlined helps to explain a number of things that have been experienced by different people. First, dreams belong to the unconscious and only occasionally impinge on the conscious mind. Second, the conscious mind is only a small part of our whole experience. When a person says that they know such-and-such, what this means is that they know such-and-such. at the conscious level. Third, many things such as extra sensory perception (ESP), hypnosis, clairvoyance, etc., arise from the relationship between the conscious self and these other selves. Fourth, given our present knowledge, we do not know how to measure and/or analyse the influence of the selves outside the conscious self. Fifth, mystical and religious experiences can be explained as a link between the conscious self and the superconscious self – or even with the collective unconscious. Sixth, 'peak experiences', when body and mind are one, arise when the conscious self makes contact with the true self or even the the higher self. Seventh, because the false personalities are well developed, it is very difficult to know what your true self is. Eighth, it is possible to develop techniques that allow the conscious self to experience these other selves. Ninth, illness, especially mental illness, can arise when conflict occurs between the needs of the various selves. Tenth – and the one relevant for our present discussion – the unconscious self, along with the superconscious and collective unconscious, have superior knowledge to that of the conscious self.

The argument being advanced here, then, is that you have a true personality which is so embedded in your conscious and unconscious selves that you are usually unaware of it. Most of your experiences are conscious experiences, but you do have the ability to make contact with your other selves (including the collective unconscious). These other selves have greater knowledge than your conscious self, and this knowledge can be drawn on by suitable methods. Your inner guides belong to the selves outside of your conscious self.

Yin and Yang

The Yin-Yang principle states that human consciousness has two complementary parts which are polar opposites: the *Yin* (the female, dark, receptive, earth, etc.) and the *Yang* (the male, light, creative, heaven, etc.). In terms of the idea being applied to thought, the Yang is the rational male intellect while the Yin is the female intuitive mind. This Chinese conception is illustrated in Figure 3.

Figure 3

Fritjof Capra (1975) describes the diagram thus:

> This diagram is a symmetric arrangement of the dark yin and the bright yang, but the symmetry is not static. It is rotational symmetry suggesting, very forcefully, a continuous cycle of movement . . . . The two dots in the diagram symbolize the idea that each time one of the two forces reaches its extreme, it contains in itself already the seed of its opposite.

It is not my intention here to go into the complex philosophy of T'ai Chi: but I wish to draw the reader's attention to the fact that we all possess both male and female characteristics, regardless of our designated sex – a point made so long ago in this ancient Chinese philosophy, but now becoming more widely accepted by psychologists. This comes out most especially in our dreams. In this mode of expression, the different personalities (as outlined in the previous section) take on separate entities and characters. Two or more persons may be involved in a scene when, in fact, it is your different personalities. Most important is the fact that some of these will be of the opposite sex to your own. Far from being pathological, this is a most natural expression of your other selves and can allow you to come to grips with difficulties you may face at the conscious level.

To summarize, within everyone there lies deep down their opposite: their female (yin) or male (yang) half. Once you recognize that there is an opposite within you, the next job is to see how you may gain from its presence.

How Many Inner Guides Do We Possess?

Do we possess no inner guides, one inner guide or more than one? To answer this question we must be a little clearer on what we mean by an 'inner guide'. An inner guide can be thought of as a person, male or female. The person can be from the past, the present or the future. They may be young or old, from our homeland or abroad. They belong to the realm of the true self, the unconscious, the superconscious or the collective unconscious – as highlighted in Figure 2. They are not a manifestation of the conscious mind. The reason for this is straightforward. It is the conscious mind which glimpses the inner guide, and so, by definition, must belong to another realm of consciousness. It is the limitations of the conscious mind in distilling the varieties of experiences that can be obtained which leads to doubts and confusion. When a person has a revelation, this is an obvious contact with an inner guide. But revelations are not the only examples of such contact.

Because inner guides belong to the areas of consciousness outside our conscious experience, they have knowledge beyond what is known at the conscious level. Furthermore, the principles which hold at the conscious level do not hold at the level of these other spheres of consciousness. For instance, at the conscious level you cannot be in two places at once. But this is not the case for the other spheres of consciousness. It is only the physical body that cannot be in two places at once. The most unusual aspect of these other spheres is to do with time. There is no past, present or future. All is simultaneous.

If one goes along with these remarks, then it follows that not only do inner guides exist, but that many exist. They are persons from the past, present or future who belong to spheres of consciousness outside the conscious sphere. They can be of either sex and can be young or old. They are extremely knowledgeable, especially about ourselves. The type of knowledge that they possess in part depends on which consciousness they belong to: whether belonging to the true self, the unconscious self, the superconscious or the collective unconscious. This in itself may be a useful piece of information. When calling on an inner guide, which we shall discuss in the next section, you can decide which sphere of consciousness you would like the inner guide to come from. It may be useful then to give some brief comments about each of the spheres we outlined in Figure 2:

The Conscious Self   This is the part of our consciousness of which we are directly aware. It consists of all our feelings, impressions, sensations, etc. Basically, it is all the information we take in from our senses – including the mechanics of analysing and processing this information.

The Unconscious Self   This complex term refers to all thoughts, feelings, sensations, etc., that go on below our level of consciousness but which influence our behaviour. Not only does it involve instinctive body functions (sometimes referred to as the lower unconscious) but also mental activities which involve the imagination and symbols.

The True Self   This is what Assagioli (1965) calls the point of pure self-awareness, and what Ouspensky (1950, 1957) calls the magnetic centre. It can be likened to a white screen which is unchanging. But our consciousness is like pictures shown on the screen. The difficulty we have is in distinguishing the screen from the pictures.

The Superconscious Self   This involves our inspirations and intuitions, our urges to do great things and the seat of our ethical values. It is the source of our feelings of altruistic love and of ecstasy. It is this sphere which we think of when referring to revelations, religious experiences and mysticism.

The Collective Unconscious   We can think of the conscious and unconscious selves (along with the true self) like a cell. This cell belongs to a greater organism from which it takes things in and to which it gives things out. So the collective unconscious is the 'liquid' (ether?) in which we find ourselves.

Calling on Your Inner Guides

In this section I wish to discuss how you can use creative visualization to call on your own inner guides. The technique itself is straightforward, but it does require a little practice. First, get yourself into the deepest relaxed state that you can, as outlined on p.10. For this particular use it is important to get as deep as possible because your inner guides reside in those layers of consciousness not so easily accessible while conscious thoughts 'cloud' the mind. Only when the mind is quietened can you even begin to approach an inner guide; and earlier attempts will be wasted.

In this sequence of visualizations we shall employ the idea of the TV screen, at least in version 1, which is discussed in more detail in Chapter 10. The suggestions can go something like this:

Version 1   In a moment I am going to switch on the TV set. When I do so I am going to see a male figure. This male figure is going to be one of my inner guides. I know that he is going to be one of my inner guides, and I know that I will be able to ask him questions about myself (or decisions, etc.). I also know that he may be from the present, the past or the future and that he may be young or old. I am now going to switch on the TV. (Once it is on wait for a male figure to form on the screen. When it does so you will be able to converse with him. This is not unusual, it is merely a method of reaching your other selves. You can ask him questions or ask for advice. Now indicate to the male inner guide that you will soon be finishing your conversation and thank him and say that you would like to call on him again.)

(When the first inner guide has gone, continue as

follows.) In a moment I am going to switch TV channels. When I do I shall see on the screen my female inner guide. I know that she will be one of my inner guides and I know that I will be able to ask her anything I want to. I also know that she may be from the past, present or future and that she may be young or old. Just as for my male inner guide, I know that she will be of great help and comfort to me. (Now switch channels and wait for the figure to form. Once clear – and it will become clearer with practice – talk to her and ask her what you want, just as if she were in the room with you. When about to finish tell her that you enjoyed the conversation, thank her, and say that you would be glad of the opportunity to talk to her again.)

Both in this version and in the next, it is important that at the end you indicate a desire for further contact in the future and that you thank the inner guide for their guidance or simply for their conversation.

In this next version we shall be brief because in essence it is the same as version 1, the only difference is the place and way of evoking the inner guide.

Version 2   I am in a rain forest and I am hacking my way through very thick undergrowth. It is hot and I am feeling very tired. I now come on a clearing and in this clearing there is a waterfall and a beautiful lagoon. I strip and take a swim, and it feels really good and refreshing. And then I lie down and rest and feel wonderfully relaxed. I then put on a loose garment, like a dressing gown, and continue to relax in the warm sun.

I then hear a male voice, it is calling me. I turn to the waterfall, and from the side of the waterfall comes a man. (You could have him pass through the centre instead.) And I know immediately that this man is one of my inner guides. (Now hold a conversation as in version 1. After thanking him and indicating pleasure in talking to him again, see him disappear into the waterfall. Then see a female inner guide also come from the side of the waterfall. Again hold a conversation, making sure to thank her and request the opportunity to talk to her again in the future.)

At any one time you need not call on both male and female inner guides. The purpose here is to indicate that each can be called in exactly the same way. More than that, it indicates that within your own psyche there is a male and female element, and these inner guides are indications of just such elements. If you are a male, you should try to hold quite a few conversations with your female inner guide, and if you are a woman then you should try to hold quite a few conversations with your male guide. The reason for this is because we very rarely let our opposite have much say in what we do and in what we say. This can lead to inner conflict, but it also means that we do not tap our full resources sufficiently. Furthermore, by calling on the opposite sex it is possible to gain some very useful information about personal relationships that you may be involved in and may be giving you difficulties. The point is that if you are having difficulties then you can consult your inner guides. Since only you will know them and only you will be talking to them, in secret as it were, then there is no need to be shy or bashful.

Depending upon the type of conversation you wish, or the type of advice you may desire, you can request a particular guide; that is to say one from your true self, from your superconscious self, or simply from your unconscious. For example, if you have difficulty with a problem that involves an ethical judgement then you call on your inner guide from your superconscious self. When doing this with the TV screen, simply say that when you switch on the TV set you will see a male (or female) inner guide from your superconscious. In the case of the waterfall, when you get to the clearing and after you have bathed, call on your superconscious inner guide to come forth from the waterfall because you need his/her help.

After some time you will be able to recognize your inner guides very easily, you will know which sphere of consciousness they belong to and what type of advice or information they will be able to supply you with. They may even bring in other persons to help you!

Caution
When receiving advice from inner guides it must not be blindly accepted. Your inner guides will give you sound

advice, but it is possible that you may get advice from someone who is not your inner guide. You should always assess the advice in terms of your conscious mind and convince yourself (conscious self!) of the soundness of the advice. With time you will get to know and trust your inner guides and this will be less of a problem. But at the beginning caution is very much in order until you become proficient at calling on your inner guides. It is very much like trying to improve your intuition and gaining more and more confidence in carrying through what your intuition indicates you should do.

4
THE PRINCIPLES OF CREATIVE VISUALIZATION

In this first part we have dealt with some of the more conceptual aspects of creative visualization. This has been necessary in order to show that imagination is not abnormal. On the contrary, it is a most normal feature of the nervous system but has largely gone unutilized because behavioural psychology claimed that it was 'unscientific'. To a large extent it was kept alive in works on magic and in Eastern philosophies. With the interest in expanded consciousness, however, there has been a return of interest. This work is beginning to show that imagery and the use of the imagination in creative visualization is grounded in sound principles.

Some of these principles and basic propositions concerning creative visualization are scattered throughout this book – in both Parts I and II. Those in Part I are largely conceptual, but the basic message is that the brain when it creates an image (whether the image is a memory or something unreal) gives rise to consistent body changes and to behavioural changes. If these changes are to be brought about then they must be impressed upon the mind when the mind and body are in a relaxed state. Only when mind and body are sufficiently relaxed will suggestions take root in the subconscious mind.

It is one thing to state the importance of images and the use of the imagination but they must be practised. Part II provides such practice.

Here the intention is to bring together in simple and

straightforward statements principles and propositions that have been made in this book. There are fifteen in total. At the end of each the reader will find where it is discussed or utilized:

1 Creative visualization is a subjective experience which uses imagery and imagination. (Chapter 1)

2 Images can take many forms; e.g. visual, auditory, motor, tactile, gustatory and olfactory, but the two most important are visual and auditory. (Chapter 1)

3 Images create corresponding body changes. It does not matter whether the image is a memory or something unreal, the response can be equally effective. (Chapter 1)

4 Images affect the body most if they are strong, clear and the person believes in their influence. (Chapter 1)

5 Imagination can be trained by training the use of the right hemisphere of the brain. (Chapter 1)

6 The will can be used to direct the imagination or oppose it. When the will opposes the imagination then it is the imagination which will govern behaviour. (Chapters 1 and 9)

7 Dreams belong to the subconscious and utilize features of the right hemisphere of the brain. (Chapter 2)

8 There is in our personality a core which is the true self surrounded by the conscious and unconscious selves. The unconscious also includes the superconscious and beyond all these is the collective unconscious. People rarely know their true self, they only know their false personality. (Chapter 3)

9 A person's personality has both a male and female component (the yang and yin) which can be called on in the form of 'inner guides'. These 'inner guides' belong to the levels of consciousness beyond the conscious level. (Chapter 3)

10 Concentration and attention can be combined (in the form of one-pointed attention) to achieve efficient behaviour. (Chapter 5)

11 Creative visualization employs goal-directed imagery to bring about desired outcomes. These can be for objects, life-styles, and desired personality traits. (Chapter 5, 7 and 9)

12 Sport can utilize creative visualization to good advantage. It is the basis of inner games and autogenic training. (Chapter 6)

13   A number of memory aids; e.g. link and peg systems, utilize creative visualization. A more recent development, also using creative visualization, is the construction of mental maps. (Chapter 8)

14   Goal-directed visualization employs many features of the right hemisphere of the brain. (Chapter 9)

15   Health can be improved by employing creative visualization. (Chapter 10 and 11)

PART II

5
IMAGERY IN
BUSINESS SITUATIONS

We begin our uses of creative visualization with the work situation. The majority of people spend a large portion of their life at work – and the housewife probably more than others. Three features of work stand out most particularly:

1 The need to concentrate and pay attention to what you are doing.
2 The need to make decisions.
3 The necessity to have good relationships with your colleagues.

We shall deal with each of these in this chapter. In addition we shall take two typical job situations, which are fairly representative, to illustrate how creative visualization can be utilized. The two we have chosen are: (i) typing and shorthand, and (ii) selling. It should be possible to combine a number of the ideas put forward in this chapter to apply to your own work situation. Even if you are a steeplejack or hairdresser, you should be able to easily adapt the ideas to your specific requirements.

Although we shall be covering a wide spectrum of topics in this chapter, they all have one thing in common: *the use of creative visualization*. It is this feature we shall be stressing, and although it is not the only feature of the business world, and certainly not the most important one, it is the one which has been largely neglected.

We begin with a discussion of one-pointed attention. The aim here is to see how to utilize creative visualization in order to be more efficient. Efficiency does not mean that you are a 'workaholic', it simply means that you utilize your time better by knowing how to pay attention and deal with one thing at a time. This naturally leads into a discussion of decision-making, largely directed at the manager; but, of course, many situations in all walks of life involve decision-making. In the next two sections we shall discuss two typical work situations: typing and shorthand and selling. Finally we shall discuss dealing with human relationships. Although we shall be concerned with relationships at work, clearly the ideas can be applied to all human relationships, both in and out of work. This final topic is an important one. Given the time we spend at work, if our relationships are not happy, then a large part of our life will not be as happy or as fulfilling as it could be. And not only the time at work; many people who have bad relationships at work bring them home!

Efficiency and One-Pointed Attention

The main purpose of this section is to emphasize the importance of one-pointed attention: how to achieve it and how to utilize it to improve efficiency in work.

Some people appear more efficient than others because they can deal with one issue at a time, and put out of their minds all thoughts of other things. If you consider this for a moment, you will realize that such people are carrying out three things. First, they are fully concentrating on the task in hand, for if they are not fully concentrating on the task in hand then other thoughts would also be going through their heads. Second, they are paying full attention to the task they are doing. Concentration and attention are not the same thing. We can think of concentration as directing a beam of light and shining up the thing we are interested in; and we can think of attention as focusing the beam of light as a lens does. A person can concentrate on a topic with his or her thoughts flitting around with no clear purpose. Attention allows the thoughts to be focused on something specific. Concentration, then, is a prerequisite for attention. The third feature is that these people are motivated; they have a purpose which brings their will to bear on the topic in which they are directing their attention and concentration. In other words, their concentration and attention is not half-hearted, it is a fully active activity. It absorbs them completely for the time they are engaged in the task. So much so that they can often be oblivious of their surroundings and to events in their vicinity. This, then, is an efficient way to undertake some appointed task. It does not matter whether the task is washing the dishes, carrying out a book review, writing a company report, typing a document, or simply enjoying yourself.

There is little point in being envious of someone who seems to be able to apply themselves completely to a task. What you need to do is correct your own behaviour so that you can do exactly the same – and even better. It is a learned behaviour and not something you are born with. Because it is learned, it can be learned correctly or it can be learned by trial and error over a lifetime. With this in mind, the purpose now is to see how to achieve this behaviour pattern and how to use it.

We shall approach this in two stages. First, we shall give a series of. instructions for actually instilling the idea of approaching all activities with one-pointed attention, and emphasizing the three features we mentioned above: concentration, attention and complete absorption. Then we shall turn to some specific situations at work to see how to apply one-pointedness in order to be more efficient.

The instructions themselves are a series of suggestions which you should repeat to yourself fairly frequently – at least once a week. These are done in a relaxed state, as we indicated on page 10. Although you do not need the exact wording that we are about to give, something along these lines will be most beneficial, and it may be worth using these verbatim in the first instance. One final observation is important. You should try as much as possible to visualize anything that indicates one-pointedness, or simply picture yourself undertaking a task and being completely absorbed in it. This aspect of creative visualization is easier to do at the second stage, but it can also be done during the first stage. So, get into a relaxed state and continue with the following suggestions:

I am going to approach each new task with one-pointed

attention. Yes, each new task I undertake, I am going to approach it with one-pointed attention. I am going to put out of my mind all other thoughts, and concentrate solely on the task in hand. Not only am I going to concentrate solely on the task in hand, but I am also going to give it my full and undivided attention. I will treat each new task as being interesting, worthwhile and deserving of my full attention. It will not matter what the task is, I will give it my full and undivided attention. I will think of nothing else except the task I am doing. For if I think of other things then I cannot be giving the task my full concentration and undivided attention, so I will put out of my mind all other thoughts except those that have a bearing on the task in hand.

And with each new task I come to I will put out of my mind any thought of the previous task or job, and also out of my mind any future task or job. For I know that to concentrate on something and give it my undivided attention means that I am acting now: that I am in the present, not the past nor the future. Yes, to approach a new task with one-pointed attention is to be fully in the present. Only by being in the present can I fully concentrate on a task and give it the attention that it deserves. And so this is what I will do.

Furthermore, I will approach each new task not with a negative attitude but with a positive attitude. And I can do this by considering each task I do as important and deserving my full concentration and attention. No task is of itself dull, hard, boring, etc, these are merely the attitudes of mind with which we approach tasks. And I know that a task will appear to me in the very manner in which I approach it. So I will approach each new task with enthusiasm and any other positive feelings that seem appropriate to the task in hand.

Because these suggestions are given to yourself while you are in a very relaxed state then they will have more impact on your subconscious mind than if you simply repeated them to yourself normally, or simply read them out. The suggestions emphasize, in particular, the three features we discussed above: concentration, attention and complete absorption in the task. At this first stage there is no obvious visualization. But this can be readily incorporated when you have a specific task in mind. Let us then turn to some task.

We shall take two: one general and one specific. The general one will simply be a typical day at work where you wish to increase your overall efficiency and deal with each task throughout the day with one-pointed attention. The specific one will be the preparation and writing of a company report. First get into a relaxed state and then continue as follows:

The efficient day

(First have some idea of what jobs you will be doing during the day. If you know what they are rank them in order of importance. Have a clear picture not only of the job but also the place where the job will be undertaken and the other people who may be involved. The more you visualize it the better.)

Today when I go into work I am going to approach each of the tasks throughout the day with one-pointed attention. I am going to start with . . . and while I am doing this I will give it my full and undivided attention. I will not be concerned with the other tasks, since I know that they will come later. I will not worry or pay attention to what I did yesterday nor what I may be doing this evening or tomorrow. For I know if I do that then I cannot be giving the task my full concentration and attention and I will then not do the job properly. And now I can picture myself doing . . . I can see myself giving it all my attention, all my concentration. I can also see myself doing it with a cheerful disposition, and seeing in it a means of self-fulfilment. All jobs, no matter what they are, can give satisfaction. And, yes, I can see myself getting a lot of satisfaction from . . .

I can now see myself finishing the first job. I can see me preparing for the second. I can see that I am putting out of my mind all thoughts of the first job and not considering the third, fourth, etc. For I know that I cannot do two jobs simultaneously, and divided attention means each is done with less than half efficiency. So I will approach each task with one-pointed attention.

(Continue through the jobs, visualizing each in the

setting in which you would undertake them. See yourself
cheerful and dealing with others in a very cheerful fashion.)

The next deals with the preparation and writing of a company
report. It is worth commenting on some of the suggestions
involved. One reason why some people are less efficient
than they may be is because they dither, or chatter or
meddle (these could, of course, be considered as three
separate reasons). Another reason is because some people
always wish to do other people's work for them: the boss who
does the work of the secretary, for instance. Finally, some are
less efficient because in any job that they do they must finish
with an elegant solution or product; this involves producing
things which have features beyond their primary function.
The point here is whether the time is better spent doing other
things which are more important. In the suggestions that
follow we shall (for illustrative purposes) assume the person
wishes to avoid all these 'faults'. First, get into a relaxed state
and then continue with the following suggestions:

Company report
(Throughout this series of suggestions picture yourself in
your office at your desk. Picture clearly the whole scene and
the people who you will consult, their replies, etc.)

Today I am going to begin my report on . . . I will
approach the whole task with one-pointed attention. Yes, I
will think of nothing else but the report, and I will
concentrate without difficulty on this report until it is done.
I will not dither. I will not delay starting it by doing
unnecessary jobs, or tidying my desk when it does not need
tidying (or whatever it is you do when you wish to delay
starting something). Nor will I go chatting to my colleagues
unnecessarily. If they wish to chat then I will make an
excuse unless it is important or unless it has a bearing on the
report I am going to write. I will refrain from meddling in
other people's business. Such meddling is merely my ego
trying to make out 'it' is important and necessary. So I will
leave others to get on with their work and I too will get on
with mine.

The report is on . . . and I am going to do a very good
report. Yes, I am going to apply myself with one-pointed

attention and carry out doing an excellent report. I will see
. . . for the relevant information, I will ring . . . for details of . .
etc. And once I have all the information I will sit down and
write. And I will find that my ideas will flow very easily
because I will be concentrating on this one thing and this
one thing only. I will not be concerned with things I did
yesterday nor things I have to do tomorrow. When tomorrow
comes I can deal with those issues with the same one-
pointed attention that I am doing with today's report. I will
be relaxed throughout the whole period of preparing and
writing the report. And because I will be applying all my
concentration and all my attention on the report I know that
it will be the best I can do. And since it will be the best I can
do, I will not be concerned about whether I could have
done it any better if . . . because I know there is no if, since I
will be already doing my best. And the best is all that one
can do.

Since I will be doing my report I will not attempt to do
other people's work. In the past there has been a tendency
for me to do the work of . . . because I consider I can do it
better than they can. But it is not my job to do this, it is theirs.
So from now on I will not waste my time doing a job that is
not mine. Anyhow, doing someone else's job will just upset
them. So I will simply concentrate on doing my report. I
will bring to bear all my concentration and all my attention
on preparing and writing the report on . . .

Nor will I require that the report be a brilliant piece of
prose, elegant and beyond criticism. If I was to do this I
would be spending an unnecessarily long time on the
report. This would be unjustified. The report is for . . .
which is basically to aid in the decision for. . . . Consequently,
it is this which must be emphasized in the report, not
elegance. This does not mean that I will present a shoddy
report. No, I shall do a very good report which is both
informative and well laid out. But there is no necessity to go
beyond this. And so I will not go beyond this.

And so, today, I will deal with this report and approach it
not only with one-pointed attention, but I shall also look
forward to writing it. I will be happy and relaxed and know
that I shall be writing a useful report and at the same time

get some self-satisfaction out of the writing.

Decision-making

Decision-making is not confined to business, and we are all engaged in decisions throughout the day – some minor and others important. Decision-making is generally an anxiety-provoking situation, and the more important the decision the more anxiety a person can encounter. We all want to make the 'right' decision, but the difficulty is clearly knowing what is 'right'. There are some obvious simple rules about making decisions.

First, obtain all the information that is relevant for making a decision. In terms of many company decisions, that usually means establishing exactly where you are at the present time (it is not always obvious exactly where you stand at a given moment in time). You need information on where you would like to be, how you can get there, and when you would like to get there. Such information is vital in any decision-making. You must know that it is feasible to get to where you would like to go, and that it is possible to get there from where you are at present. Even if all these were possible, it is still important to know that you can get there within a feasible time period. It is no good making a decision based on something being feasible – but can be achieved only in fifty or more years!

Many decisions can be aided by considering alternative strategies or plans. Each will involve some direction (even if it is to do nothing and remain on the present course). Often such strategies involve merely altering the values of certain key terms (parameters), but each alteration leads to major differences in the outcome. It is not surprising that in many business situations this type of process involves flow charts, networks, etc. All visual aids are very useful in helping the mind absorb all the relevant information. It is important that these aids do show, however, the relevant information – such as timing, constraints, resource implications, etc. For more manageable decisions, i.e. decisions that can be made by means of information that can be set out on one sheet of paper, mental maps are also a good visual aid (these are described in more detail in chapter 9). Even when the decisions are major ones, it is possible to concentrate on the crucial issues by reducing them to information that can be contained in one mental map. This has the advantage that you can sit and *see* your problem. You can *see* the crucial variables, you can *see* where timing is going to be a problem, etc.

Before we consider the creative visualization feature of decision-making it is important to note that there are four DON'Ts:

1   Don't make decisions about irrelevant things.
2   Don't make a decision too soon.
3   Don't make a decision that cannot be turned into action.
4   Don't make decisions that someone else should make.

We have now reached the stage of having all the relevant information at our disposal, and we have in mind the four things we should not do. Supposing, then, there is a relevant decision, which must be made now, and it is a decision that you have to make.

The significant point about decision-making is that once all the information is ready then there is no point in delaying making the decision. More than that; since we know that decisions are anxiety provoking, then it is important to get on with the decision so as to reduce the period over which you will feel anxious (since if the decision must be made, then you will inevitably be feeling some anxiety, which cannot be avoided). Furthermore, this is the time for the anxiety. Not when you are collecting the information, since then there is nothing you can do. Nor once you have made the decision. You then live with the outcome (unless the decision is proved to be wrong and is reversible). The point here is to have confidence in your decision, on the argument that, given all the relevant information, you made the 'best' decision – 'best' in the sense that if you had to make the decision over again, with exactly the same information, then you would make exactly the same decision. Notice that this is not the same as making a decision which is shown, in the light of *new* information, to be the wrong decision. No person can deal with information that they do not have. Life will always throw up situations where your decisions will, in the light of future information, be shown to be erroneous, wrong or even disastrous. But these are outside your control and there is no point in worrying about such things. What you must do is be prepared to make new decisions in the light of the new information.

So, then, how can creative visualization help in decision-making? The most crucial point is that an important decision should be made when you are as relaxed as possible. You amass all the information and have it ready at hand – especially charts, maps, and diagrams. You then achieve a relaxed state as indicated on page 00. You then proceed in three steps:

Step 1   (While in a relaxed state you proceed with the following suggestions.) In a moment I am going to open my eyes and look through all the information that I have for making my decision. When I do this I will be very relaxed and free from worry or anxiety. I will let my mind float freely over the material, knowing that it will search out the important aspects of the problem. It will see clearly interrelationships and all necessary points which will aid me in my decision. Most particularly, I will consider any alternative strategies so that I am familiar with them, although I will not at this point make any decision about which appears best.

Step 2   You now open your eyes and go over the material you have amassed, paying particular attention to charts, maps and any diagrams – sufficient so that you can picture them in your mind's eye. You do not even attempt to make a decision at this point, all you do is familiarize yourself with the material. If there are alternative strategies, make sure that you become familiar with these.

Step 3   Return to a relaxed state with your eyes closed. Now imagine that you make a choice out of the possible ones you have identified. (It need not at this point be the one you finally choose, simply one of the list. The intention is to go through the list one at a time.) Now visualize your future in terms of this particular choice: what it means for you personally, what it means for your division, section, company, etc. If you will be very personally involved in whatever choice you make, then ensure that you also picture in your mind's eye what type of feelings you will likely have. Now do this with each choice in turn.

When you have completed all possible alternatives then you should be more able to make a choice, and the 'right' choice. The visualization of the future, in particular, should help in trying to see through the implications of your choice.

Although this creative visualization to decision-making is not infallible, it is better than simply taking the decision without trying to deal with all the information. Where the gain comes is in taking the decision in a relaxed state and in picturing the future as it would be had you made the decision. This is very much the basis of certain therapies. It does not have to be a business decision either. To take a totally different example to illustrate the value of the method, suppose you were considering to have a vasectomy. This is an irreversible operation. You may think that it is the 'right' decision to make. But one method to help make the decision, and only one I might add, is the use of creative visualization. You could get into a relaxed state as above and then imagine you had decided on the operation. Then think through your life thereafter, most especially how you would feel and how you might react to your partner in the future. The more important the decision, the more important it is that you utilize anything that can aid in the decision-making and so reduce the anxiety both during the decision and, possibly, in the future as a result of the decision.

Before leaving decision-making, one final point is worth making. *Decisions must be followed by action.* There is no such thing as a decision that involves no action (even if it means a course of action that you are presently following). Once the decision is made then the appropriate action should be carried out. The one thing you do not do is worry about whether you have made the right decision. You have done your best in coming to terms with all the information, and that is the 'best' you can do. So have confidence in your decision and put it into action. More than that, enjoy putting your decision into action. Do not think backwards, rather approach the action with the same one-pointed attention which we discussed in the first section of this chapter.

Typing and Shorthand

I want now to turn to a very practical application of creative visualization. Many people engage in either typing, shorthand or both. With modern technology there is less need for shorthand, although this cannot be said of typing. With the growth of word processors, this feature of modern business will become even more important. I shall first take shorthand and then typing, since the visualization in each case is somewhat different.

Shorthand

Shorthand, and I shall assume it is Pitman Shorthand that is being learnt, is based on phonetics. The phonetic alphabet must first be learnt, and there is no substitute for this. Once the alphabet is mastered then it is a case of practice and putting the alphabet into use. Shorthand, besides being phonetic, is a very visual language. It is this feature which can be utilized in creative visualization, and is not stressed sufficiently in shorthand courses. Take my own Christian name, which I shall use for illustrative purposes, this is represented by:

Now this is very easy to hold in your mind's eye. It is even more effective if you simultaneously have a picture of what the word means. For example, you might have this symbol dangling above my head, with my face very clearly pictured in your mind. The basic point is when learning you deliberately visualize the words and sentences.

Suppose you put some time to one side for improving your shorthand. You could utilize creative visualization as one of these sessions. How would it go? First you prepare your material and lay it out ready. One possibility which can be very useful here is to place on index cards a word or sentence, and have a whole series of these. The procedure is in two stages. First, get into a relaxed state and then continue with the following suggestions:

Stage 1   In a moment I am going to open my eyes and look over my shorthand. I am going to be very relaxed and I am going to concentrate with one-pointed attention. I will find the words and sentences will be easy to learn and that the pattern in the language will be clear and obvious to me. I will find no difficulty writing the strokes and distinguishing the thin from the thick strokes. Very soon I will be able to dispense with the vowel symbols because I know that most words are clear from their consonants.

Also I will take my cards and I will look at the words (or sentences) on them. My mind will absorb the information in them very easily and quickly. What I shall do is simply look at the cards, with no deliberate effort to memorize what is on them. I shall be very relaxed and calm. And I shall turn over the cards quickly, and this will speed up each time I go through them. And I know that my right brain will be picking up the relevant information which will help me in the future to learn and be able to reproduce the shorthand.

When I come to write the shorthand I will find that I can remember the symbols very easily. I will find that I will be able very quickly to match the stroke with the sound. My thick and thin strokes will come very easily because my hand and fingers will soon know exactly the right pressure to put on in order to achieve these strokes.

Stage 2   You now open your eyes and go to your work area and go through the cards and practice reading and writing shorthand.

Another session could be put to one side for simply picturing in your mind's eye individual words written in shorthand. See the word or sentence very clearly. Even better, combine the symbol with what it represents. Since this is purely a practice session you can choose words with obvious pictorial representation; chair, piano, man, woman, telephone, etc. The sheer effort of doing this will make it easier in the future. You will find as you walk along the street you can turn objects you see into their shorthand equivalent, and picture the shorthand equivalent in your mind's eye. It undoubtedly becomes easier with practice.

Typing
There are two aspects to typing: speed and accuracy. Both require to be present. Greater speed at the expense of accuracy

is not necessarily more efficient than a slower speed with greater accuracy. There is one other important consideration which any typist knows is important: typing with a relaxed body posture. If body posture is wrong, or if you type in a tense fashion, then very soon your muscles will ache and your typing speed will slow down and your errors increase. In what follows we shall deal with all three:

1 Speed
2 Accuracy
3 Relaxation

We shall take two different types of sessions. In one you simply engage in *Inner Typing*, but do not actually do any typing (very much like *Inner Games* we shall discuss in the next chapter). In the second session you give yourself suggestions as to how you will type when you open your eyes. In each case you first get into a relaxed state, and continue with the following series of suggestions:

Inner typing
(Picture yourself at a typewriter or word processor, sitting very relaxed and poised ready to type. Then as the suggestions continue carry out visually all that is being said in the suggestions.)

I can see myself at the typewriter. I am typing a very long report (book, or whatever). I am very relaxed and comfortable and I begin typing. I can *see* and *feel* my fingers going quickly over the keys. I don't have to think about what I am typing, my fingers just move quickly and easily over the keys. My typing is not only quick but it is very accurate. Yes, I am making no mistakes at all. I can *see* the pages being typed one after the other. The pages are mounting up as I begin to type still faster. I am whizzing along faster than I have ever seen anyone type before. My fingers are moving at lightning speed across the keyboard, and yet at all times I am accurate and very relaxed. In no time at all the report (or whatever) is complete. I feel very satisfied with my work and my boss (or whoever) is very pleased with such a quick, accurate, and well laid out report.

Suggestions for actual typing

In a moment I will be practising my typing. I will sit at the typewriter and feel very calm and relaxed; and this calmness and relaxation is going to remain with me for the whole period that I am typing. I will find that my fingers will move faster and faster over the keyboard. Yes, my fingers will move faster and faster. And not only that, but I will be very, very accurate in my typing. There will be very few, if any mistakes. I am going to be a very quick and accurate typist. My fingers will move without me being consciously aware of it. My fingers are light and dextrous and will simply flash along the keyboard with no difficulty whatsoever. I will be very relaxed at all times and happy. I will be typing with one-pointed attention and concentrating wholly on the typing and nothing else. And I know that I will be pleased with my results. And in the future my typing is going to become quicker still, quicker and more accurate. Yes, while I am typing in the office (or wherever) my typing is going to speed up and yet remain very accurate indeed.

Even in this second series of suggestions it would be useful if you actually visualized yourself doing the typing and *seeing* and *feeling* your fingers moving quickly and accurately over the keyboard. You should find no difficulty in *feeling* as well as *seeing* this. Typing is a very spontaneous action which has largely been relegated to the right hemisphere of the brain. These suggestions, and most especially the 'Inner Typing', is appealing to your right brain. You should have no difficulty visualizing yourself at the keyboard and seeing the typed copy. In the case of a person using a word processor the visualization should be easier still, since the CRT can readily be pictured in your mind's eye. In this case you can combine the feeling of your fingers whizzing across the keyboard and simultaneously seeing line after line of typing come up on the CRT. Furthermore, if you happen to find word processors daunting, then you can adapt the creative visualization to overcome this!

Selling

A great deal has been written about selling, and there are a number of courses one can attend in order to improve one's technique and ability. In this section the only intention is to highlight how to use creative visualization as an aid to selling. One reason for choosing this topic is that it is very amenable to creative visualization. Furthermore, once it has been seen in this context it can readily be adapted for other occupations. readily be adapted for other occupations.

The main points that are to be emphasized are conviction, self-confidence, and success. What runs through all the suggestions is a series of positive statements. If you happen to have a particular negative attitude (such as not being able to sell more than x policies in any period) then these should be incorporated in the suggestions in such a way that they are eliminated. We shall illustrate this with just such a mental 'block'. You can, of course, readily replace this with your own if you happen to have one.

First get into a relaxed state. The suggestions can then go something like this:

I know that I can sell x. I know that I can convince people that x is necessary and that it is important for them to have it. I will have no doubts about the product itself. It is not for me to deny its usefulness. On the contrary, given I have decided to work for company y then it is important that I put all my effort into doing a good job. Since this job entails selling x then I will put all my energy and all my enthusiasm into selling x.

If I do not have confidence in the product and in myself then this will come across to whoever I am trying to sell it to. So I must believe wholeheartedly in the product and have no doubts whatsoever about it, and about my ability to sell it. And I *do* have confidence in myself and in my ability to sell. In fact, I am the most successful salesman in the company, the country, the world!

I can now see myself going up to a house (person, or whatever). Yes, I can see myself carrying out a fantastic sale. I can see myself confident, convincing and in full control of the situation. I can see myself overcoming any objections the person has, no matter what it is.

I no longer believe that I can only sell . . . of the product. That is simply a mental block which I have created myself.

There are no 'blocks' in reality; all 'blocks' are mental and created by people. I no longer have any such mental blocks. I have confidence in myself and in my ability to sell as much as the situation dictates.

(Now visualize yourself going from one sale to another, each concluded with success and each sale bigger than the one before.)

The suggestions can be extended and adapted to your own requirements. What is essential is to picture your success. See yourself going from one sale to another. See yourself going through the motions in as great detail as possible. Always see yourself as very confident and very successful in what you are doing. Not only see yourself, but *feel* your success. Feel the situation being in your control, feel the elation of having carried off a masterful sale. But do not stop with just one sale. Go on to bigger and bigger sales – bigger than you have ever had, bigger than any of your colleagues, bigger than you thought possible. Possibilities are for the rational left brain. The process you are engaging in is a right brain stimulation. So exaggerate, fantasize.

Human Relationships
In this final section we shall deal with the use of creative visualization in human relationships in the work situation. Almost all, if not all, people who work have to work with other people. No matter how enjoyable a job is, it can become tiresome, unfulfilling, or simply downright miserable if human relationships break down. This can occur both in work as well as in the home.

The first thing to realize, or accept, is that you cannot (or should not?) change other people. All you can (or should?) change is yourself. The second thing to realize is that when something that someone does is annoying then the *annoyance is not in the thing being done, but in your response to the thing which is being done*. Things and actions are not in themselves annoying: the annoyance is within ourselves in response to the thing or action. In work situations the most usual problem is when our egos are 'hurt'. We get annoyed at the shop steward, the boss, the teacher or whatever because their attitude is such that it diminishes the importance our ego has attached to ourselves. We get annoyed at decisions because they do not go exactly the way we (our ego) would want them to go. Someone makes impertinent remarks, or even loses their temper and we retaliate (again the retaliation depends on the extent to which the ego feels threatened). The message, then, is that generally, annoyance in a work situation results from a feeling of being threatened – where the threat is felt certainly at the subconscious level, but also possibly at the conscious level.

Even where the ego does not feel overtly threatened, human relationships can be improved in a work situation by deliberately going out of your way to be helpful to others, or simply just to talk to others in a friendly way – no matter how obstreperous or uncooperative they may appear to be. This simply means maintaining a happy disposition within yourself no matter how others react. This partly comes from self-confidence, but also it comes from feeling relaxed. The reason is that relaxation brings with it contentment. *Relaxation and annoyance are opposites*. You cannot be relaxed and annoyed or angry at one and the same time. Hence, the more you practice being relaxed at all times and in all situations, the more content you will be.

The object of creative visualization, therefore, is to create a feeling of relaxation in the work situation; to create a suitabale response to those with whom you have to work with and for. The following series of suggestions can act as a guide. First get into a relaxed state, as indicated on page 10, then continue as follows:

In the days to come I am going to feel very relaxed at work, I am going to feel very calm and relaxed throughout the day. No matter what happens and no matter what others may say, I shall at all times remain calm and relaxed. If criticism is called for, then I shall do so in a calm and relaxed manner. Nothing will annoy me; no one will annoy me. I know that annoyance is within myself, and the only one to suffer from annoyance is myself. This is wasted energy and will only leave me feeling unhappy. So I shall not get annoyed, I shall not let other people get me annoyed. I will at all times feel calm, relaxed and happy. (Continue this and embellish the suggestions in terms of your own job and the people you have to deal with.)

I can now see myself at work. I am very calm and very happy. No job is beneath me. If the job has to be done, then I go ahead and do it. And I can see myself getting on so well with the people I work with. Yes, I can see that I am getting on very well with.... Even though in the past I may not have always got on with . . ., I can now see that the situation has changed totally, and that I am getting on very well with.... No longer do they annoy me. Even when they lose their temper (or whatever) this in no way interferes with my calm relaxed state. If they wish to get annoyed that is their affair, but I am going to remain relaxed and calm at all times. (Not only see this but feel it happening.)

I can now see myself getting on very well with.... Yes, I can see myself talking to them, feeling very calm and relaxed and getting along very well. And because I am relaxed I can see that they too respond in a much more friendly way. Yes, I can see the two (three, or more) getting on very well indeed.

From the suggestions given above it is clear that the object is to embellish the suggestions with pictures of your work situation – the room, the people, and anything else that is relevant. It is important to keep the suggestions positive and the pictures full of relaxation and confidence. See yourself doing and saying the things you want to say. Above all, feel the feelings that are consistent with the pictures you are creating. It is important that the pictures are accompanied with the emotions consistent with them. By doing this their impact will be that much greater, and will have more effect on your behaviour. By creating in your mind's eye the behaviour you want, then this has more chance of actually occurring because of the influence these pictures and suggestions have on your subconscious mind. This is the message of this chapter and all the ones that follow.

6
CREATIVE VISUALIZATION IN SPORT

In this chapter I wish to consider how visualization can be used to improve a person's sport. You need not be a budding Olympic champion, merely a person who wishes to reach your full potential in a particular sport – or even in all sports that you undertake.

Traditionally, sport has been looked at from a purely physical point of view, but it is now becoming clear that greater performance, and certainly greater satisfaction, can be achieved when mind and body are in accord with one another. In the first section we shall, therefore, point out the limitations of training and the over-concentration on equipment. In the following section we shall look at how some individuals have turned to the use of psychoanalysis as a means of improving their game or performance. We shall then discuss the importance of the correct 'mental set' and see how some sports personalities have made their own individual attempts to find a suitable mental set. We shall also discuss the importance and role of the coach. Some remarks are also given on the now popular (at least in the United States) *Inner Games* and the use of *Autogenic Training*. It will be shown that these have in common the use of creative visualization. In the final section, therefore, we shall outline specifically how anyone can use creative visualization as a means of improving performance.

The Limitations of Training and Equipment

In nearly all sports, training and the right equipment are essential. There is no substitute for training, and there never will be. You cannot sit in an armchair and achieve skill! But training, too, has its limitations. There are two completely opposite points of view as to whether you can over-train. One point of view is that you can never train enough and that you should push yourself (or be pushed by a coach) beyond what you think is your endurance. The basic reason why this is successful for some people is that they have too low an idea of their own potential. By being pushed beyond endurance they come closer to their 'true' potential. The opposite point of view is that you can over-train, in the sense that your training can involve incorrect responses which then become programmed into your nervous system, and so you constantly repeat the same mistakes.

Of course, both of these can be correct. If a person does have a low expectation of their performance then over-training may give them confidence and allow them to raise their actual performance closer to their potential. At the same time, over-training may increase the number of incorrect responses; if repeated so often that they become programmed into the nervous system, they may be hard to eliminate. In fact, then, the training may be required to undo what the training had formerly done.

The most usual response to poor performance is more training and more lessons. But very often lessons are rigid and follow a fixed format. This means that not enough flexibility is incorporated into the training sessions. It also means that the mind becomes closed to new ideas. The lessons become routine and consequently do not often achieve their stated purpose. In this respect lessons and training tend to be overrated. The reason why they are still so highly rated is that there appears to be no alternative.

One other main limitation of training exists. Many sports require high degrees of concentration and attention. Generally, training is not given in these very important attributes. Often more attention is paid to equipment than to improved concentration and attention.

It is clear that the right equipment is important in many

sports, but even here there is greater limitation as a means of improving performance by this means. But even in sports like tennis, there is a limit to how far a better racket can improve performance.

The conclusion we draw from these remarks is that training and the right equipment are very important, but that after a certain point these are not enough. Furthermore, training tends to be too rigid and concentrates almost exclusively on the body and ignores the mind. Sport is not simply the performance of the body. *Sport involves performance of mind and body.* Maximum performance can only be achieved when mind and body are in co-ordination – are one. This realization has led a number of sports personalities to turn to psychoanalysis as a means of achieving greater performance.

Psychoanalysis in Sport
People who engage in sport know that their performance varies according to how they feel and how they approach their game, or whatever. They realize that mind and body must co-ordinate. But how? It is when questions like this are asked that sports people turn to psychoanalysis.

One such example is that of soccer player Steve Archibald. He was helped, both in his game and out of it, by two psychologists – John Syer and Christopher Connolly. He was so impressed that he reckons very soon that most big-time clubs will not only employ a physiotherapist but also a psychologist. In his case performance was improved by visualizing great intensity moments that he had gone through in the past. By doing this he could call on the experience in the future. The cricketer Mike Brearley has also undertaken psychoanalysis. He began this in 1979, shortly before his tour in Australia, and resumed it again on his return – although five visits a week does seem a bit excessive! In his case, the visits have not made him 'analytical'; on the contrary, they have tended to encourage spontaneity. In addition, they have enabled him to recognize different varieties of attention.

At the moment these are isolated cases, but there is a growing awareness of the role that psychologists and psychoanalysts can play in improving individuals' games. The major problem is that psychology and psychoanalysis are little understood by many sports personalities, and consequently there is much resistance to them. But psychology and psychoanalysis are partly to blame for this. There are many varieties of each and sports people want to know the right ones. Unfortunately, there are no right ones. This means a choice must be made. But psychoanalysis need not be undertaken if all that is required is an improved performance. What many of the psychoanalyses have in common, especially when dealing with motivation and performance, is the use of creative visualization. In a later section we shall indicate how you may employ this technique without having to visit a psychoanalyst.

The Correct Mental Set in Sport
The ice skating champion Robin Cousins has said:

> When I get changed, I have developed this habit of doing everything right first. My right leg into my trousers first, my right skate on first, and I tie up my right lace first. I even step on to the ice right leg first.

This is an example of someone creating a *mental set* for themselves. Basically, a 'mental set' is a state of mind that a person finds right and allows them to reach their full potential because it allows them to approach the game, or whatever, in the right way. In general terms it is simply 'psyching themselves up'. Almost all sports people attempt to psyche themselves up. Billie Jean King is known to have done this before her tennis matches and Duncan Goodhew, the Olympic swimmer, does it also. These are by no means isolated incidents. Weightlifters do it before each lift, and in their case you can actually see it in operation.

Not all mental sets take the form of a ritual, as in the case of Robin Cousins, but ritual is by far the simplest technique for creating one. Some mental sets deliberately use visualization techniques, as in the case of Duncan Goodhew, who before each swim lays down and after closing his eyes visualizes the swim to be undertaken in very fine detail – even to the extent of feeling the water. Others, as in the case of Daley Thompson, rely on relaxation techniques which are suggested in works on self-hypnosis and autogenic training.

Mental sets can be both positive and negative. A typical

negative mental set is created by psychological limits in a number of sports. For a long time, four minutes remained a psychological lower limit for fast runners of the mile. It was believed that this could not be done, until accomplished by Roger Bannister. A more revealing psychological upper limit was that of 500lbs in weightlifting. Again, it was believed that this could not be exceeded. It was broken by Valery Alexis by being 'fooled' into believing that he was lifting less than 500lbs when, in fact, it was just over this weight. The importance of these illustrations is the fact that belief, along with training, plays a role in performance. Training is absolutely essential, but, as Daley Thompson has said:

> The only limitations are mental: you can do anything you want, and the guy who thinks most positively will win.

But positive thinking needs cultivating. Furthermore, it is not clear what is meant by 'positive thinking'. How does one go about thinking positively?

Creating a right mental set is basically activating the right hemisphere of the brain. But not only that, it is establishing a relationship between the right and left hemispheres of the brain, in such a way that they do not conflict with one another. This is the basis of 'inner games', which we shall deal with in the next section. The rituals that many people go through when they engage in sport is a means of achieving this relationship. But it is unstructured and without form. It is often established by trial and error.

What, then, must a correct mental set achieve, or deal with? There are basically five aspects it must deal with:

1 The environment
2 Faults in technique
3 Mental limits
4 Relaxation
5 Competitive attitudes

Every sport is done in a particular environment, whether it be outdoors or indoors, whether in courts or in/on water. You cannot usually change the environment. The correct approach, however, is to ensure that the environment has the minimum adverse effects on your performance. If you happen not to like the umpire then you do not want this to hinder your performance. If you happen to have had an argument with someone just prior to performing, you do not want this to upset your performance. The list is long, but all it means is that your performance should not be adversely affected by your environment. The use of creative visualization, which we shall show in the final section, can deal with this problem.

We pointed out in the first section that it is possible to overtrain. Alternatively, it is possible that training is creating faults, even if not over-done. Such faults must first be noted. But having noted them, there is the difficulty of knowing how to correct them. Some of these types of faults are quite frustrating. The person knows that they have such a fault, but repeatedly carry it out. Even training does not seem to eliminate it. In fact, the repeated training may lead to even greater frustration, since the lack of success becomes more obvious. It is at this problem that 'inner games' are specifically directed.

Mental limits, personal mental limits especially, generally lower performance. They act like a barrier. They are invariably psychological barriers and, as such, cannot be eliminated by more training or by logically analysing the problem. They require a different technique altogether. Creative visualization, being a right brain function, is well suited to this task.

There are many forms of relaxation techniques. What is required in sport, however, is the facility to relax for short spells between performances, or just before performing. Progressive relaxation, which begins with the feet (or head) and then progresses slowly through all the major muscle groups, is very therapeutic, but it is hardly suited for sports people. What is required is a method that can establish relaxation quickly, that can be done while sitting, lying or even standing. Although creative visualization is not the only way that this can be accomplished, it is one worth cultivating.

Finally, we come to the question of the right competitive attitude. This will vary from person to person and from one sport to another. Suppose you lack the competitive spirit that is claimed to be so necessary in a number of sports. You may even know this. But what can you do about it? Training cannot give you a more competitive spirit! Again, it is a mental state and so a mental technique is called for. Visualizing yourself being more competitive is one such method.

Each sport is almost certain to have its own best mental set; and even for any given sport it is certain that the 'best' mental set for one individual will not be the same as for another. So little attention has been given to mental sets that individuals have had to find their own by trial and error. Such a person as Duncan Goodhew has gleaned information from a variety of sources and has evolved his own approach. His case is a good illustration of the difficulties that can be encountered by trying techniques designed for other purposes. Many relaxation techniques have very specific instructions on breathing. But in swimming, the breathing rhythm is tied very much to the stroke. In the case of Daley Thompson, the decathlon champion, the variety of events does not readily lend itself to a single technique. Having read a variety of sports analyses and techniques (probably self-hypnosis or autogenic training) he has developed his own approach: the most important being his ability to relax between events.

For professional sports people the coach can play a very significant role in creating the right mental set. In broad terms they provide three functions:

1 Help
2 Faith
3 Knowledge

Their role in helping with the acquisition of skill and their role in training are well attested. But where they generally fail is in developing the necessary mental attitude, and consequently achieving the full potential, of their protégé. This is quite understandable because they are not trained psychologists. Even so, sport is very much the co-ordination of mind and body. If a coach simply concentrates on the body, to the exclusion of the mind, then he or she is only doing part of their job. It is quite straightforward for a coach to learn how to use creative visualization and to help his or her protégé to use such visualization to their best advantage.

Inner Games and Autogenic Training
It is not the intention of this section to supply detailed instructions in inner games and autogenic training, but rather

to give a brief account of these two developments and to indicate that what they both have in common is the application of creative visualization. Although I will only discuss these two, creative visualization is not confined to these alone. It plays a major role in Gestalt psychology (see, for example, Perls, Hefferline and Goodman (1951)), and most especially in psychosynthesis (see, for example, Assagioli (1965) and Ferrucci (1982)). Inner games and autogenic training, however, are both used by sports people and so they will give us some insight as to how to use creative visualization in sport.

Inner games has been developed in the United States, most especially by W. Timothy Gallwey. The ideas were first laid out in his book *The Inner Games of Tennis* (1974) and followed up in a later book (with Kriegal) on *Inner Skiing* (1977). His latest book, *The Inner Game of Golf* (1979), develops his ideas still further. Gallwey does not profess to have developed a new idea. What he has done is show quite convincingly that the subconscious mind must be brought into the act of aiding in performance. More than that, he has demonstrated that very often poor performance is a result of conflict between the conscious and the subconscious.

His approach is to argue that a person is composed of two selves, which he calls Self 1 and Self 2. Self 1 is the analytical self and is constantly giving instructions to Self 2, who is not involved in talking but is simply performing. Self 2 is more the instinctive self. Gallwey denies that Self 1 and Self 2 can be equated with the left and right hemispheres of the brain, but all his analysis indicates that this is so. Self 1 is the egotistical self. Its constant analysis and talking leads to tensions in the body, which in turn lead to errors and poor performance. Training, as we highlighted above, tends to feed only Self 1.

In many ways his advice is *not to try*, to simply let go. Trying too hard simply leads to mental and physical tension, conflict and over-tightness. What he is suggesting is to have more faith and confidence in Self 2. A good example of this is supplied by Liz Ferris, a former Olympic diver. In the USSR two Soviet experts adjudged perfect one of her one-and-a-half reverse somersaults. This particular dive was, for her, a 'let go'. In her practice sessions she had failed to achieve the dive successfully and so on the occasion she expected to flop. The result was that she relaxed and let go. In Gallwey's terms, Self 2 then took over and allowed her body and mind to co-ordinate. This oneness between mind and body has been experienced by a number of sports personalities. But such 'peak experiences' can be felt by everyone. Joggers with no particular desire to be sporting enthusiasts, have occasionally had experience of lightness and freedom where things slow down and there is complete harmony between mind and body. On these occasions they feel as if they could jog on and on without tiring.

The strength of Timothy Gallwey's books lies in supplying exercises and approaches to develop confidence in Self 2. Until one recognizes the existence of Self 2 then there is no thought of training it. It is here that creative visualization comes in. The inner game, as its name implies, is basically the act of carrying out the game, or stroke, etc., in your mind's eye. Of course, this must not be undisciplined and haphazard. It must deal with such things as concentration, awareness, confidence and willpower – all of which are dealt with in the books just cited.

Autogenic training was an outgrowth of self hypnosis and auto-suggestion. Some people just did not seem to respond to the process of hypnosis. Whatever the reason for this, it was found that many of these people could still respond to suggestions made by themselves when in a relaxed state and with their eyes closed. In many respects the state is very like light hypnosis. Developed in the 1920s by a German psychiatrist, Johannes H. Schultz, it is only now becoming more widely used in Britain and the United States.

The basic technique relies on a relaxed body state which is then given auto-suggestions, the phrasing and order being important. Both in its basic form, and in its more advanced forms, visualization plays a very important part. To see this let us take the basic form of autogenics, based on the work of Dr Karl Rosa (1976). This concentrates on six body parts in the sequence given. These are:

1 *Right arm*   Heaviness in the right arm (left if left-handed) is suggested. Visualizing it being made of lead helps, although any visualization will do.
2 *Right hand*   Warmth in the hand is suggested. Visual-

ization in the form of sunlight or a warm fire helps to illicit the required response.

3 *Pulse calm and strong* Constant suggestion that you are calm and relaxed and that the heartbeat is slow, steady and strong.

4 *Breathing calm and regular* Constant suggestion that breathing is calm and regular.

5 *Warmth in the solar plexus* The solar plexus is a little above the navel. It is an important centre and responds well to suggestions of warmth. Visualize a sun at this point radiating warmth and health-giving rays.

6 *Cool forehead* Repeated suggestions for a cool forehead. Visualization takes the form of a scene where the body is warm but the forehead is cool (but not cold).

It is clear from this list that autogenic training is very similar to the progressive relaxation given as an introduction to all the training sessions suggested in this book, and outlined on page 10. The major difference is the order in which things are done and the more frequently warmth is illicited. The use of creative visualization, however, is most important. It is possible to repeat by means of words the suggestion for a part of the body to become warm. But words are a left brain function. Unless these words activate some response in the right hemisphere of the brain, then they are unlikely to have any effect. A far superior way of activating the right hemisphere of the brain is to visualize a scene which will 'naturally' illicit warmth. Visualization may be ordinary, but it can be made even more effective still if it is creative – if it is imaginative. We shall take up this point in the next section.

Although autogenic training is largely designed for relaxation, it can be used for suggesting other things. Once the sequence above has been completed then it is possible to progress on to other auto-suggestions concerned with, say, your particular sport. The inner game can be tagged on to the autogenic training, so combining the two techniques.

Using Creative Visualization
The first four sections in this chapter basically justify the use of creative visualization as a means of improving performance in

sport. It is now time to be a little more specific on how to go about using such creative visualization techniques. Since this topic is vast we shall deal here only with training, performance on the actual day, improved confidence and psychological limits. It is, however, possible to adapt these visualizations to other aspects, such as dealing with the environment and improving one's competitive spirit.

Training

First, get into a relaxed state as described on page 10. This should not be rushed because this in itself will be very beneficial. It can be enhanced by incorporating the autogenic exercises given above. This relaxation should not be under-estimated. We generally do not relax, in the strict sense of the word, and so our bodies do not know how to 'let go'. These relaxation exercises can be engaged in frequently as a means of learning to 'let go'.

In this series of auto-suggestions it is assumed that you are going to be going to the gym to do a basic training exercise. It can, of course, be adapted to your own specific needs and sport. Throughout you should *visualize* every detail, *feel* yourself going through the exercises, *feel* the muscles and the emotions. The auto-suggestions can go something like this:

I am now going into the gym to do my training, I am going to go through a standard set of excercises and I am going to do this with enthusiasm and a realization that these excercises are going to make my body supple, strong and better in every way. I am going to concentrate solely on the training and on nothing else. My concentration is going to be better than ever before and my mind and body are going to harmonize as never before.

(Now picture yourself going through each exercise. As you do so keep up the suggestions. Suppose, for example, that you are going to begin lifting weights and then go on to the bench, which you are going to step on and off.) I am picking up the weights and they feel very light. I can feel them toning up my muscles. I can see that my breathing is correct and that I am relating my breathing to the movement of the bar. I can feel a surge of delight as I feel my mind and body attaining a harmonious relationship. I am now going on to the bench. I am stepping on and off. I can feel no tiredness in my legs. My breathing is easy and steady. I can feel myself obtaining a rhythm which co-ordinates my legs, my breathing and my balance. And I am enjoying the exercise because I know that it is toning up my body and making it supple and strong so that when I need to strain it it will be able to achieve what I want . . .

This is a very realistic scene. It is very like the inner game technique, except here the purpose is simply to *see* and *feel* yourself going through a typical routine. This can be readily adapted to some specific routine that you may wish to go through. Suppose for instance, there was a skating routine you wished to practise, you could simply get into a relaxed state and go through it in your mind's eye. While doing this you would make suggestions just like those given – most especially auto-suggestions of a perfect performance, one where mind and body are one. You should feel yourself do the perfect performance, and feel the elation of having done so.

Performance
This leads us quite naturally into dealing with performance. In dealing with this it will help if we take a specific example. Suppose we take the high jump. The object of these auto-suggestions is two-fold. First, to visualize the actual event, and second, to exaggerate 'beyond the reasonable'. Why carry out this second aspect? To visualize the actual event and actual performance is very useful, and certainly utilizes the right brain rather than the left. You are not, however, utilizing the right brain efficiently. The right brain does not work on logic and realism, it works on symbolism and synthesis. Symbolism is best achieved by pictures. More than that, the more dramatic the pictures the better the response will be. It is this creative use that requires exaggeration. There is a difference between visualization and creative visualization! Creative visualization is imaginative – and even possibly bizarre. Visualization is realistic and simply duplicates reality in the mind's eye. It is the creativity which is largely missing from the inner games and autogenic training.

So let us take up the high jump. You can, of course, replace it by anything else.

I am now making myself ready for the jump. I am running up to the bar, I have the right pacing and the correct momentum. I rise from the ground and clear the bar with a perfect jump. My body is angled correctly, I clear the bar with no difficulty and I land correctly. The bar is now being raised and I go through a second jump. This is even better than my first. I can now feel that I am getting into my stride. I am finding that my body and mind are co-ordinating as they have never done before. Nothing seems to matter to me except clearing the bar. There is just me and the bar. (Continue for as many notches as you like. But make sure that you finish on a notch higher than you have ever gone before.) I can see the bar being raised to a higher position than I have jumped before. But I feel that everything is going right for me and that I shall have no difficulty clearing the bar on this occasion. I am now running up, and, yes, I can feel that my whole body is working harmoniously and that my mind and body are one. And, yes, I clear the bar with ease. It was such an exhilarating feeling. (You may even go higher still.)

(We now come to the creative part – the exaggeration.) I am now with a special party of athletes. We are going off to the moon for a special Interplanetary Olympics. I arrive and I am to do the high jump. I change and am now ready for my jumps. And I know that it is not going to be the same as on earth, because the moon has a lower gravity than earth. In fact the jumps are not metres high but miles high, and it is not bars to jump over but mountains! And I now begin and I clear the first mountain with ease. I feel myself light and my movements graceful and correct. The second and third mountains, too, I have no difficulty with. And I now come to the highest mountain. This peak has not yet been jumped, but I feel that today I can clear it with no difficulty. I feel good, and my body and mind are harmoniously balanced as never before. And I now begin my run, and, yes, I clear the mountain!

I now return to earth. I am to perform in yet another event. But I feel so good because of my performance on the moon, I feel that nothing on earth is of any difficulty. And this is so. I run up and clear the bar with no difficulty at all. I still feel light from my stay on the moon, and I feel so integrated and so co-ordinated.

By now you should get the idea. Notice, in particular, that in the latter part of the suggestions, the same feelings you had on the moon are retained when you return to earth. Also notice that the auto-suggestions include ones specifically about being harmonious and being one, with mind and body co-ordinating as never before. In terms of the inner games, this is asserting the importance of Self 2 and establishing a harmonious relationship between Self 1 and Self 2.

Confidence

Lack of confidence in sport arises from self-doubt, negative attitudes and psychological limitations which have been self imposed. When concentration is solely on Self 1, to use again the idea of the inner game, then there is too much reliance on the analytical. Self 2 does not get an opportunity to express itself. The same errors are repeated, and the person often knows that he or she is repeating the same errors. This leads to annoyance, anxiety and increased tension, which in turn leads to yet more poor performance. So a vicious circle is set up. Trying, in the usual sense, will most likely make things worse. When in such a vicious circle you must stop trying. You must let Self 2 express itself.

In addition you can engage in creative visualization as a boost to confidence and a means of instilling a positive attitude. A positive attitude and greater self-confidence are quite general concepts, but here we shall concentrate on applying them specifically to the sporting context.

Get into a relaxed state as described on page 10. The auto-suggestions can then go something like this:

From now on I am going to think positively about my sport. I am going to eliminate all doubt and all worry. Doubt and worry merely sap my energy and serve no useful purpose. Each time I have a negative thought from now on I shall say to it, 'Go, I don't want you'. Yes, each time I have a negative thought I shall tell it to go. And I know that with time these negative thoughts will get less and less, because they will have nothing to feed on. By banishing them and not allowing them to stay in my mind, I will not be supplying them any energy. And because they have no energy they will be replaced by positive thoughts. I will be thinking about good things. I will know that my sport is going to improve, that my training is going to get better, that my game (or whatever) is going to get better and that I will find that my mind and body will become one. (Now we come to the creative visualization.)

Version 1   I can now picture the air going into my lungs as I breathe. Yes, I can picture the health-giving oxygen passing from my lungs into my body and the carbon dioxide passing out of my body, into my lungs and then being expelled as I breathe out. And now I can see all my negative thoughts being attached to the molecules of carbon dioxide. Yes, the carbon dioxide is attracting all my negative thoughts like a magnet. And I can see them very clearly passing into my lungs and then being expelled from my body. (Keep these suggestions up for a while.) And now I can also see that positive thoughts are being attracted to the oxygen molecules. And as I breathe in, these positive thoughts are being transferred from my lungs and into my body. Yes, they are infusing every part of my body and mind. (Keep these suggestions up.) And now I can see that all negative thoughts have been expelled from my body and that my body is infused totally with positive thoughts. (Try and see your body as if it were transparent and the positive thoughts like little red granules – basically anything that allows you to picture the resulting positive thoughts in your body.)

Version 2   Yes, I can see a dam where water has built up behind it. This water is dark – dark because it contains all my negative thoughts which have been building up over the past. And now I can see the floodgates open and the water flowing out. Yes, all the dark water is flowing out and taking all my negative thoughts with it. (Keep this up until you are satisfied that all the water has been let out.) And now I can see clean water filling up behind the dam wall. Yes, this water is clean because it contains positive thoughts in the water (see anything, even fish can represent the positive thoughts.)

It is possible to follow these suggestions about positive thoughts with the next on creating greater self-confidence. Alternatively, you can engage in this next one on its own.

> I can see a cloud, a sort of mist, enveloping me. This cloud is a very strange cloud because it is, in fact, an organism that 'feeds' on anger, guilt, self-doubt, suspicion and all such thoughts that lead to lack of confidence. And, yes, I can see this cloud drawing from my body all these feelings, all these feelings of doubt (or whatever the major difficulty is). Yes, I can feel the cloud drawing them through the pores of my skin. And now I can see the cloud moving off and I feel fantastically free – free from anger, free from guilt, free from doubt and free from suspicion (or whatever). Free to let Self 2 express itself. Yes, I feel that now I can relax and let my body and mind unite as never before. And I know that this will make my game so much better.

We now switch to a totally different scene, which is to follow the one just given without coming out of the relaxed state. In this scene you are to have a special object – a magical object. This should either be an outfit, such as a tracksuit, or something to do with your sport, such as a racket. In these suggestions I shall assume that it is a tracksuit.

> I now take out my special tracksuit, my magical tracksuit. Yes, this tracksuit allows me to be just what I want to be, it allows me to be just what I should be, and allows me to do just what I want to do. In this suit I am supremely confident and know that there is nothing that I cannot do and more than that, it allows my mind and body to become one.

Psychological limits

Finally we come to how to use creative visualization to deal with psychological limits. These are purely mental barriers and as such cannot be eliminated by training, nor very often by logical reasoning. Psychological limits are usually associated with subconscious thoughts, accordingly a totally different technique is called for. Creative visualization is well suited for this job. Emphasis is, to repeat, on creativity. We begin with a straightforward visualization followed by a creative visualization. Begin by getting into a relaxed state. To illustrate the technique

I shall assume that the sport is running.

I am now preparing for my race. I feel today supremely confident. My breathing, my muscles and my mind feel harmoniously balanced and I feel as one. And now I am off. Yes, I can feel that my rhythm is just right. And the speed of. . . is not a barrier. I know that all barriers have been broken in the past. And I feel that today I can break this barrier also. I now come to the finish of the race and I hear that I have broken the record! There are cheers and shouts and everyone is tremendously pleased, and so am I.

I am now on the operating table. I am having my legs replaced by bionic ones. These allow me to run as no one has ever run before. Yes, with these bionic legs all barriers can be eliminated, all records broken. And now I can see me having my bionic legs tested. I am running with a counter machine at the side and I can also see how fast I am running. And the feeling is tremendous. And now I am in a race. I begin and very soon I leave everyone else behind. I have no difficulty at all in breaking all previous records.

It should be noted in these suggestions how use is made of creative visualization. As repeatedly mentioned, it is possible to use visualization, but this does not take full advantage of right brain features. It is like doing a job with only one hand when two are available!

7
OVERCOMING SHYNESS

In this chapter we shall be concerned with shyness. This is not an easy topic to deal with and here we shall not be concerned with all aspects of shyness, especially excessive shyness. Our aim is more limited. We shall in the first four sections discuss various aspects of shyness. This is vital if we are to arrive at a method of dealing with it; but at the same time, we shall not be considering all possible solutions to this social difficulty. We shall then concentrate on how to use creative visualization as one method of approach.

This chapter draws on the work of Philip G. Zimbardo (1977). Anyone interested in the broader aspects of this problem would do well to consult his book. The intention here is to highlight some of the more obvious aspects of the problem which will, at the same time, help to improve the use of creative visualization. In the first section we shall discuss some of the consequences of shyness. This will be followed by an important distinction: general shyness as compared with shyness arising from specific occasions. We shall then consider some of the causes and correlates with shyness. These initial sections will allow us to see what changes in lifestyle are necessary if shyness is to be overcome. These first four sections will then help us to consider how to tackle the problem with the help of creative visualization.

Consequences of Shyness

Although it is very difficult to define shyness, and we shall not even attempt to do so here, leaving it to the reader to come up with his or her own interpretation, the consequences are pretty obvious. At the same time they are so diverse that any attempt to put them into categories is very difficult. Some broad generalizations are, however, quite useful.

When a shy person finds him or herself in a situation where he or she feels shy, one of the first sets of reactions are physical in nature. The heart may begin to beat faster, perspiration may increase, blushing will invariably occur and there may be 'butterflies in the stomach'. The significant and tell-tale sign of shyness is blushing, since this occurs in no other situation except when a person feels shy. It is unique to the emotion we label as 'shyness'. People, of course, react differently to shyness and one or more of these physical reactions may be uppermost – but most occur together. Other reactions, less physical in nature but having physical manifestations, are saying very little (or even nothing) and being inobtrusive. It may even have the opposite reaction, namely, talking excessively and not pausing to think, especially of what other people are saying. Both of these, whether talking too little or talking too much, are problems of communication. They are not the only aspects of this difficulty. As the anxiety increases for the shy person, thinking becomes confused and the person often says things he or she does not mean. He or she cannot think quickly and when forced to do so finds that his or her mind becomes 'a blank'. This hints at a very crucial aspect of shyness. People are not shy about objects, to be shy is to be afraid of people. Shyness occurs when in encounter situations. But even more than that, a person can be shy when on their own simply by imagining what they may be like when they have to deal with some encounter or another. This may be so great that they avoid the encounter altogether. If this applies to every encounter the result is that the person is afraid to go out of the house.

The difficulty of facing up to encounter situations very quickly leads to related difficulties. These may include such difficulties as making friends, meeting new people and having new experiences. It may also lead to the prevention of speaking up for one's rights or expressing one's own opinions and values. This in turn leads to a shy person's strengths to be poorly evaluated by others. For the shy person themself, it can lead to negative feelings of depression, anxiety and loneliness. A vicious circle is created for which the shy person sees no obvious escape.

Two Types of Shyness

Shyness is not only quantitatively different, it is also qualitatively different. It can vary from feelings of awkwardness in the presence of another person to traumatic feelings of anxiety. Through this continuum there are a variety of types of anxiety. But we can distinguish two types which will help us later. First, there is the generally shy person. Such a person seems to be shy in all circumstances where other people are involved. They find meeting people very difficult, and will either avoid the situation altogether (which in the case of a child is usually in the form of disappearing and hiding) or will feel very anxious to the extent of saying very little unless asked a direct question. The anxiety remains, and may even increase while the other person or persons remain. Social occasions, in particular, are a great anxiety-provoking situation. This shyness arises from a lack of confidence in social skills, or simply a lack of self-confidence. This usually involves the person having difficulty in starting a conversation and also keeping the conversation going. This can even arise with people they know very well, such as members of their own family and/or with acquaintances – but most especially with strangers.

The second category of shy people are those who are shy only in very specific circumstances or with very specific people. Although their physical reactions tend to be the same as those for the generally shy, they are less dramatic and are not as long lived. Some examples may help to distinguish the two. For instance, a lecturer who is not shy talking to large audiences about his special topic may be very shy when giving a speech at a wedding. A person may be only shy with members of the opposite (same) sex. A person may be normally confident but extremely shy when involved in intimate encounters. There are numerous other examples. The basic point is that most people are shy in some context or other. When a person says they are never shy, ask them how they would react if they were asked to visit the Queen or the Pope?

In the second category, the specifically shy, it could be argued that 'shyness' is not the correct word to describe the situation. It could be said that such people merely exhibit a degree of 'discomfort', the actual degree varying according to the specific event in question. But this simply highlights the difficulties with definitions. Discomfort could be said to be a mild form of shyness! But even for these people, it can still be a problem if the event in question is a frequent one, such as every occasion you talk to your boss.

As Zimbardo (1977) rightly says, shyness is not all a question of disadvantages. Some people may find advantages attached to being shy. Shyness can be linked to such positively thought of attributes as 'retiring', 'unassuming' and 'modest'. In some circles it may even be taken as a sign of being 'sophisticated' or 'high class'. To the extent that a person may find pleasure in solitude, shyness increases personal privacy and so increases this eventuality. Shyness allows friendships to be carefully selected and therefore more likely to be long lasting. By allowing the possibility of anonymity it also allows a person the opportunity to be themselves more frequently, or at least not engage in behaviour that they think they 'ought' to do and 'should' do. In the final section we shall make particular use of this anonymity feature as a means of liberating the 'true' personality.

The important feature of this section, at least in the light of the methods we shall adopt in the final section, is that it is necessary for you to establish whether you wish to overcome general shyness or shyness of specific events or occasions. The methods for overcoming each are not the same. It is not simply that general shyness is quantitatively greater than specific shyness, it is also the point that general shyness is qualitatively different from specific shyness, and as such requires to be approached in a different manner.

Causes and Correlates of Shyness

Shyness arises from a lack of self-confidence, either a general lack of self-confidence or simply a lack of confidence in a particular event or occasion. In the second case the event or occasion is quite clear; even so, carrying out some of the suggestions below will help in getting to kr ow your shyness in some detail. That is the purpose of this section: to get to know your shyness in as much detail as you can.

It is no good simply admitting that you are shy. That is too vague and does not help in the process of overcoming shyness. You must know in detail when you are shy, what brings on the shyness, whom brings on the shyness, the costs and benefits of shyness to you, whether shyness is associated with actual events or hypothetical events, and the degree to which shyness has caused you not to take risks and lost out on things as a consequence. This step is essential if you are going to change your lifestyle: a necessary change, as we shall indicate in the next section.

You should investigate your shyness as if it belonged to someone else; in other words, try to be objective when assessing it. We shall in a moment list a number of things you can do in order to come to a full understanding of your shyness – and it is *your* shyness and no one else's which must be scrutinized by you. It should not be thought, however, that they are trivial and you can dispense with them. In one sense they are trivial, but you must spend time on your shyness if you are going to eliminate it (or reduce it). Suppose, by way of analogy, you had a problem with your car. Would you simply leave it unattended and hope it would correct itself? First, you know that it would not correct itself unless you did something. Second, you would either work on it yourself or take it to a garage. In the case of your shyness you may be able to consult a psychiatrist but more generally you would attempt something yourself – or you may be like many and do nothing about it, in which case it will not improve.

Here then is what you can do – you need not attempt all of these but the more you attempt the better you will understand your shyness:

1 Keep a *shyness diary*.
2 *Make a list* of all the things that make you anxious – also record whether these are actual or hypothetical (i.e. being anxious about some event which just might happen).

3 *Record exactly how you respond in shy situations* on the list you have made for 2, or make a separate list. Your physical responses and your responses to other people. Also record how you think other people are responding to your shyness.

4 *Write yourself a letter* on how you believe your shyness developed. Add to this as memories return, or as you gain further information about its development.

5 *List the costs and benefits.* Take a piece of paper and divide it down the centre. Enter on the left (or right) the costs attached to your shyness and on the other side the benefits you may derive from shyness. Give some careful thought to the benefits because these may not be so obvious but are, all the same, very real.

6 *Make a list of all the people in the past who have rejected you or your ideas in any way.* Associate with each name the thing that was rejected then rank the rejections from the most distressing to the least distressing. (Do not underestimate the importance of carrying out this ranking.)

7 *Make a list of all the occasions in the past where a risk was involved in some choice situation.* Divide the list into two parts: (a) those where you accepted the risk, and (b) those where you passed up the risk. Further sub-divide (b) into those risks you passed up which you were glad that you did, and those for which you were sorry that you had done so.

8 *Analyse why you may be lonely.* (We shall provide one method in the final section.)

A Change in Lifestyle

Once shyness has developed it will not go away on its own accord, like some of the somatic illnesses. To repeat the analogy we gave in the previous section, suppose your car had a problem. Unless you do something about it the problem will remain. So, too, with your shyness. Even analysing it, as we suggested in the previous section, will not in itself do anything to correct it. But this raises a very vital point right from the outset. Can shyness be eliminated or reduced?

There is a common, and very destructive myth, that shyness cannot be eliminated, that shyness is a part of the character – the unchangeable part at that. One extreme form of this type of argument is that shyness is an inherited characteristic. The present writer does not subscribe to such a view. Shyness is environmentally determined. You learn to be shy, either generally shy or shy in just some circumstances. If one of your parents is shy then it is probable that you will (subconsciously) take on a similar behaviour pattern. This does not mean that you are genetically shy, rather it means that your behaviour pattern has been influenced by your family setting. Even if your parents are not shy, if in your early childhood you became shy, they may not have known how to help you overcome it and so the shyness remained, or even developed still further.

You must believe that you can correct your shyness, wholeheartedly believe that you can correct it. This is an essential first step in the programme of recovery. Without this belief you will be making the recovery unnecessarily more difficult – if not impossible.

Once you have convinced yourself that you can, in fact, correct your shyness then the next stage is to realize that this implies action. You must put in some effort. Although an obvious thing to say, it is vital. It is easier to remain shy than to change. To remain shy involves you in no effort. Of course, it also means that all the difficulties associated with shyness will remain. *To eliminate shyness requires a programme of action.* It requires persistent effort, and effort that will be required over a long spell of time. You cannot eliminate shyness overnight. Again this is important to appreciate. Many people can put great effort into some enterprise but cannot sustain this effort. Eliminating shyness is not a means to an easier life, but it is certainly a means to a better and more fulfilling life.

Five changes in lifestyle are necessary in eliminating shyness. Let us first list them and then discuss each of them in turn. They are:

1 A change in the way you think about yourself.
2 A change in the way you think about your shyness.
3 A change in the way you behave.
4 A change in the way you consider the way other people think about you.
5 A change in the way social values promote shyness in you.

1   Generally a shy person thinks of themselves as no use,

incapable of doing something or coping with something. This can arise from a variety of sources, but is often instilled by some incident or series of statements made to a person – most especially a child. If someone is told repeatedly that they are 'stupid', or some such phrase, then very soon they behave as if they are. This is often the case with the shy person. At the beginning they have difficulty with something or other and become self-conscious. If something is then said then this may sow a seed which over time begins to grow. This can even be a single incident. Take the case of a young man who, on his first intimate encounter, is told in a sharp tone that 'he is incapable of satisfying anyone!' Such a situation could lead to shyness from then on in every such similar circumstance. The point being emphasized with these examples is that such shyness is environmentally created. It is not that a person is inherently no good or incapable of doing something, they have merely convinced themselves that this is so. The change that must be brought about is the realization that *anything that has been created can also be destroyed* – that there is nothing in their 'true self' (see Chapter 3) which would mean that they should be the way they are.

2   This brings us very close to changing the way you think about your shyness. A shy person is often concerned about making mistakes and consequently feeling humiliated. But humiliation is a feature of the ego and not of the true self. Over time the ego has been fed with negative feelings and behaviour patterns and is consequently strong and well formed. Making mistakes only 'hurts' the ego but not the true self. Given that the ego is generally too well developed, what a shy person must realize is that it is important that the strength of the ego be reduced. This means accepting the possibility (and inevitability) of making mistakes. Realizing that the only one to be 'hurt' is the inflated ego and that this must be reduced. This act of reducing the ego will at the same time strengthen the will.

The ego is also involved in the privately shy. A privately shy person is worried about feelings while a publicly shy person is worried about behaviour. For the privately shy person the feelings being aroused are being done so by the ego. Take rejection. A shy person dislikes being rejected, and this is often one reason why they will not perform some act or other (e.g. ask a person to dance). But who is being rejected? It is the false personality created by the ego which is being rejected. It is 'this' which feels hurt by the rejection. In the case of the publicly shy person, such a person must realize that other people's views are of no real consequence to them. If, for instance, you commit some social indiscretion then this will normally go unnoticed or will only elicit a passing comment. If people harp on the indiscretion, then it is they who have a problem and not you.

Another feature of shyness which must be changed is that shyness involves negative thinking. Negative thoughts seem to be held far easier than positive thoughts – why this should be so is not easy to ascertain. Furthermore, negative thoughts utilize the imagination very readily, and most usually at a subconscious level. Not only are positive thoughts harder to fill one's consciousness with, but to incorporate the imagination in them requires an act of will (which is not a contradiction in terms). Thus a shy person must recognize the negative nature of their thinking and replace such negative thoughts with positive ones. They must see how the imagination is utilized in their negative thinking and use it purposefully in their positive thinking.

3   Overcoming shyness requires a change in your behaviour. Most shy people recognize that one of the major things that leads to anxiety is talking to people, whether strangers or even members of their own family. Having recognized this, however, then it is vital that something is done about it. It requires a deliberate behaviour which has been carefully thought out, and has built into it a sequence of acts from the least disturbing to the more disturbing. To the shy person, 'jumping in at the deep end' is not the way – and is more likely to lead to drowning than to a solution. To illustrate the point: you may decide that for the next week you will talk to one new person each day. You may decide to begin with the local shopkeeper. Some rather innocuous comment will do to begin with. You may then turn to the local librarian. On the third day you can talk to someone in the shopping queue or bank queue. As the

week goes on, you can become more adventurous and speak to a total stranger on a bus. In carrying out these acts it is very important that you realize that at the beginning you will make errors and blunders. But these will not be important because the conversations themselves are not important. The people you happen to speak to are not important to you. You can only gain confidence by doing something often enough. Ask anyone who appears confident in some situation and you will probably be surprised to find that at the beginning they, too, were very shy or anxious, and that this diminished with more repetitions. This is reasonable. Think back to how shy you may have been to eat out in a restaurant, but that this became less the more times you went into a restaurant. Look on other anxious events in the same way, as no more than the fact that you have not repeated them frequently enough. Realize that with time this anxiety will diminish. Do not make each event unique. Assume it is one of a series, each giving you more confidence to deal with the next.

4   To change the way you consider how other people think about you, it is important to realize that this involves only dealing with public shyness. We mentioned this under point two above. The change that is required here is the realization that other people are more concerned about themselves than about you! It must be realized that we all make mistakes and still survive in the world without having to withdraw from it or run away and hide. The change is not in others, but in the way you think about the way others think of you when you do something wrong, clumsy or silly. It is a change in behaviour. For the shy, however, these 'social graces' can cause great anxiety and shyness. Rather than accept some formal invitation to something, the shy person is likely to conjure up all sorts of possible errors, mistakes, etc., to such an extent that he or she turns down the invitation. This is a classic example of the force of negative thinking and the power of the imagination. The change in behaviour is to turn the negative thoughts into positive thoughts. Rather than see the event as a means of disclosing your inefficiency, it should be looked on as a means of self-improvement. It truly is a matter of your way of thinking. The event will be the same, but it can be a challenge

or a nightmare. Which of these it is is purely a matter of your own mentality. If it is a nightmare, then it is important that you realize that your mentality is not unchangeable. It can be changed, and to this we now turn.

Using Creative Visualization

Having discussed shyness in some detail we now turn to creative visualization as a means of dealing with it. Although not the only way, it is a very useful means of coping with this problem. It also has the advantage that it can be done at home in your own time. We shall deal with four visualizations:

1 Breaking down *barriers* that prevent the achievement of specific goals.
2 Eliminating *negative thoughts*.
3 Considering your good and bad points by means of a *duplicate*.
4 A means of dealing with *loneliness*.

It should be noted that these do not deal with shyness directly, but rather deal with aspects associated with shyness. Furthermore, for the specifically shy person, i.e. for the person whose shyness is only associated with a specific person or event, then one and two will be the most useful. For the generally shy person, however, all four will be useful.

Barriers

A shy person often has barriers that pervent him or her from attaining goals. At the same time, shy people often do not formulate their goals specifically enough. In any attempt to deal with barriers, therefore, you must formulate your goals as clearly as possible (see Chapter 9 for a more detailed discussion of goal-directed visualization). Make a list of these and think about them frequently. We can picture the situation by means of Figure 4. (see page 94).

As we can see from Figure 4, the barrier prevents the shy person from achieving their stated goal. The figure does, in addition, draw our attention to three very important aspects: (1) the *goal* to be achieved, (2) the *method* of achieving the goal, and (3) the *barrier* that prevents the goal being achieved. The

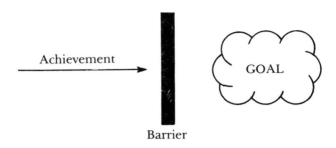

Figure 4

earlier sections in this chapter dealt, to some extent, with the methods of achieving your goal. Here we shall concentrate on eliminating the barrier.

The first job is to picture your barrier in some way or other. It can either come to mind by just thinking about it; or alternatively, you can deliberately think of it in some way – such as a brick wall, a dam, a hurdle, a fence, a bridge, a pass, a ravine, etc. All these examples conjure up in the mind a barrier or hurdle that prevents you from going from A to B. You must also discover whether there is more than one barrier. If you consider there is more than one barrier then take them one at a time, beginning with the smallest. If there are more than one, associate each with a picture indicating their importance; e.g. a small barrier can be thought of as a hurdle while a large barrier can be thought of as a ravine.

Now get into a relaxed state as indicated on page 10. Formulate in your mind's eye as clearly as you can your goal and the barrier. For the moment concentrate more on the barrier. Now begin a series of suggestions like the following – here we shall assume you have two barriers: one represented by a brick wall and the other by a ravine.

I can see before me a brick wall which is in my path. This brick wall is preventing me from getting what I want, or going where I want to go. It has been there for a long time. But I am no longer going to let it stop me. I have with me today a means of breaking down the wall. I have brought with me a handgrenade. I now pull out the pin and throw it at the wall. It is most effective. The wall crumbles and leaves a big hole for me to get through without any difficulty at all. I now climb through and see before me the very thing I wanted (or where I want to go). And I feel very elated at having blown down the wall and am now able to achieve the very thing I want to achieve.

I am now in the country, a vast open space. I come on a ravine which seems to allow no way across. It is preventing me from going where I want to go. But I decide not to give in so easily and begin to search for a way across. I move along the ravine, and after some miles I come across a rope bridge where the ravine narrows. Although I have never crossed over a rope bridge before, I know that this will be my only means of reaching the other side and reaching my goal. I take a deep breath and begin going across. (Picture this as clearly as you can). Before long I reach the other side feeling elated and overjoyed at my success. I know that that was my last barrier and that my stated goal is now in sight. In fact, I can see it clearly. At long last I can see my goal and am overjoyed.

Whatever the barrier you picture the object is always the same: first to picture it and then see yourself overcoming the obstacle. The more imaginative you are the better. For instance, in the case of the ravine, rather than being so realistic in your visualization, have some enormous bird come and pick you up and take you to the other side, or have Pegasus (the winged horse of mythology) come fly in and you climb on his back and are taken to the other side. In the case of the wall assume that the wall is merely an illusion and that you take a tablet which shows that the wall is an illusion and so you simply walk through it!

Negative thoughts

Negative thoughts are not unique to shy people, but shy people do have very strong negative thoughts and so it is important that these are dealt with. Because negative thoughts are so pervasive in our society we shall give a detailed visualization to deal with this (see also the section on confidence in Chapter 6). First get into a relaxed state as described on page 10.

What I am now going to say is going to go deep down into my subconscious mind, very deep down into my subconscious mind. It is going to affect me at all times, both during the day and during the night, that is to say, these suggestions are going to affect me at all times.

These suggestions are going to sink so deep down into my subconscious mind that nothing will eradicate them, because I want them to remain there for all time. And because these suggestions are going to go deep down into my subconscious mind, then they will also influence my conscious mind too.

From now on I am going to avoid all negative thoughts. All negative thoughts are going to be eliminated totally from my way of thinking and they are going to be replaced by positive thoughts. More and more thoughts from now on are going to be positive, and any negative thoughts are going to be replaced immediately by positive ones.

Version 1 I am now imagining that the letter 'N' (see a large N in your mind's eye) stands for a negative thought and the letter 'P' for a positive thought. I can now see the negative thought, the letter 'N', being wiped out and replaced by the letter 'P'. I can now see a whole line of 'P's and 'N's, like a line of soldiers, all representing my previous thoughts. Below this line I can now see another line consisting only of a series of 'P's, and this second line represents what my thoughts are going to be from now on. Yes, all negative thoughts have been replaced with positive thoughts, and I know that as a consequence I will feel better, feel more confident and feel more secure.

Version 2 I am all black, I look as if I have just come up from a coal mine. All my skin is black and it is in my hair and all parts of my body. I then suddenly realize that this is not coal dust, it is simply my negative thoughts infusing all of my body and making it black. No amount of washing appears to do anything to the blackness. So I go into hospital. I am connected to a variety of machines, but seem to be quite comfortable. I can see one tube in particular which seems to have a black liquid in it – and so it does. This liquid contains all my negative thoughts which are being drained from my body, just like blood is taken from someone. And as I see more and more of the liquid drain off and begin to fill a large container, so I see that my body is beginning to change colour. It is becoming lighter and lighter. (Keep this up until you see no blackness in your body.)

And now I can see them connecting another tube to my body. Yes, this is filled with light-coloured liquid. And I hear the medics say that this contains positive thoughts and positive suggestions. It is a very special and powerful substance which is always very effective. And I can now see this liquid pouring into my body. It seems to give it a feeling of power and energy. It makes me feel good, happy and satisfied. Yes, nothing now seems to depress me, nothing seems to have a dark side to it. I feel revitalized and rejuvenated.

If your psyche happens to throw up a visualization of your own negative thoughts, then use this. It is always better to use an image of your own than one created by someone else.

Duplicate

This idea, taken from Zimbardo (1977), can be most effective. The idea is that you discover a sinister plot by a mad scientist to create an exact duplicate of yourself. The duplicate, however, is evil (a sort of Dr Jekyll and Mr Hyde). Since you do not want to be mistaken for the evil duplicate you must convince others of your uniqueness. As this will be particular to you we shall only begin the type of suggestions that you can undertake. Again, get into a relaxed state as outlined on page 10.

I am in a court room. There are two of us in the dock: me and my duplicate. I know he/she is my duplicate but the mad scientist made such a good copy that the jury are not sure. I know that I am not evil like my duplicate, but he/she keeps deceiving the jury. It is now my turn to take the stand and I know that I must convince the jury of my uniqueness, that the other is a duplicate copy and that I am the true person.

(Now present your evidence to the jury. If you like, imagine that you can present the jury with scenes from your past on a video. Describe these and see them in clear detail. Take as long as you like. Remember, however, that your duplicate is evil and what you are demonstrating is your good points, those aspects of your personality that make you unique – which cannot possibly be captured by a robotic double. Bring to your defence anyone who may be aware of your unique qualities.)

Loneliness

The idea of this imagery is to consider yourself snowed in for a weekend in some retreat. You are alone but have sufficient water and food. The place you are staying has everything you may want in terms of games, pens, paper, etc., but no TV, no radio and no telephone. You are now to imagine how you would spend your weekend to make it interesting and joyful. We shall not present a series of suggestions for this, but the purpose is to see in your mind's eye how you would deal with forced loneliness, but where you have everything at your disposal that would make it interesting and enjoyable. This may be difficult at first, but once you have had a few attempts at it it will indicate to you how you may now deal with your loneliness. You do not have to wait until you are snowed in!

8
IMAGERY AS A MEMORY AID

Memory is one of man's most important mental faculties. Without memory we could not learn from experience and we could not develop language; in fact, we would have difficulty engaging in any intellectual pursuit. Without experiences and language life would be very fruitless indeed. But given the importance of language and experience, many people congratulate themselves on their poor memory! How often do we hear someone excusing themselves with the phrase, 'Sorry, but I have such a poor memory!' Sometimes this is with regard to names, other times it is with regard to facts, like the time for meetings. But whatever it is, it remains an excuse to be lazy. But lazy in a bizarre sense. We forget where we put something because we do not make an effort to remember where we place it. But then we spend long periods busily trying to find the thing we put somewhere. People seem prepared to spend long periods finding things they have forgotten, rather than spend the time improving their memories.

The major emphasis of this book is that we all possess a great deal of potential which we fail to tap. The extent of memory is a classic example. People are too often prepared to accept their poor level of memory. But memory, like so many things of the mind, is something which improves with using. To use the memory properly requires you to know exactly how memory works. But scientists do not know exactly how memory works. They have, however, found out quite a lot of useful information about memory which can be used to improve it.

In the first section we discuss briefly the issue of short-term versus long-term memory. Some people have a bad short-term memory but a good long-term memory. What, if anything, is the difference between these? We next consider the fact that people remember things better if they pay attention. In addition, even if information is retained in the mind, the problem is usually that of recall. Having laid the foundation we can turn to those features of memory which utilize creative visualization. We discuss briefly the two most popular memory aids, that of the peg system and the link system. Both of these systems utilize, not surprisingly, techniques of creative visualization. But these are not the only means of aiding memory. The reason why creative visualization works is because it utilizes the holistic features of the right hemisphere of the brain. Another aid which is less well known, but equally useful, is that of mental maps, which we discuss in the final section.

It is not the intention of this chapter to supply a series of techniques for improving memory. There are a number of books written on this subject, such as Lorayne's *How to Develop a Super-Power Memory* and Dineen's *Remembering Made Easy*. The intention here is to highlight those features of these systems which utilize creative visualization. It will be apparent in our discussion that these same features occur in all the other applications we are discussing in Part II of this book. This should not be surprising since they merely illustrate how to use an obvious technique to reach the potential that we all possess.

Long-Term and Short-Term Memory

Suppose you are about to make a telephone call to someone or somewhere unfamiliar. You look up the number and then begin to dial the series of numbers (or press the appropriate sequence of buttons). For the short interval you retain the number in your mind, sometimes saying the sequence over to yourself until the dialling is complete. Having completed the task you then promptly forget the number. This is an illustration of short-term memory. Information is stored for just a short time until the task for which the information was required is complete. The holding of the information is aided along by repeating it, by a process of rehearsal. This process is immediate and the information is in immediate consciousness. Long-term memory, on the other hand, deals with information about events which are long past. The basic difference is that long-term memory involves the person bringing into conscious awareness the material which is stored somewhere in the brain (where that 'somewhere' is is not known and may even involve the whole brain itself).

Evidence suggests that short-term memory is limited. It appears to be limited to a small number of items – some put the number as (the magic) seven, others a little smaller. But what comes out of these investigations is that it is the number of 'chunks' which are limited, not the information stored in each 'chunk'. To give a simple illustration, consider the sequence 1357 246. Now this is composed of seven bits, seven digits to be precise. You could remember each digit in turn as a means of remembering the sequence. Alternatively, you could consider the number as three chunks, 13 57 246; or as two chunks, 1357 246. You may even ignore all the numbers and remember the pattern in which they are formed – all the odd numbers to seven and then the even numbers! Short-term memory, therefore, is limited to a number of bits of chunks, but each bit can be composed of chunks (no more than seven) in its own right.

Investigations into long-term memory find that there appears to be no limit to it – contrary to popular opinion (excuse!). In order to get from short- to long-term memory the information must be retained sufficiently long for this retention to occur. Once in long-term memory the problem is then to retrieve it, to recall it into conscious awareness. We shall take up the issue of retention and recall in the next section. What is important is that the capacity of the long-term memory is unlimited. Nearly all of our learned experiences, including language, are stored in long-term memory. The idea that you can 'fill your head with too much information' does not appear to be the case. As Russell in *The Brain Book* puts it:

Memory is not like a container that gradually fills up, it is more like a tree growing hooks onto which the memories are hung. (Page 106).

Furthermore, the more memory is used the easier it is to store yet more information. It appears that the more you use your memory the more hooks there are to hang the information on, and because there are more hooks the 'best' hooks are chosen.

The information contained in this section can be seen in terms of Figure 5.

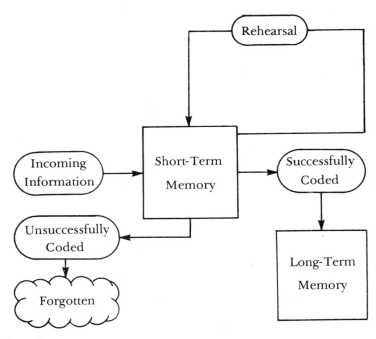

Figure 5

Attention, Retention and Recall
In Figure 5 we note that incoming information must first be retained in short-term memory. Furthermore, it must be coded successfully if it is to pass into long-term memory. In both of these distinct processes attention plays a most important part. We remember best what we pay attention to. This is

almost so obvious that we do not realize its importance. When something is outstanding we remember it quite easily. Why is this? It is simply that anything outstanding or unusual attracts our attention. We can walk down a street and see but not observe. We observe when something 'catches our eye', when we direct our attention to something outstanding or unusual. Seeing does not involve attention, this is involved only when we observe.

We have from this an immediate clue to memory. We tend to remember those things in which we are interested. To be interested in something means that we pay it attention. We remember things least when we are not interested in them. Thus the schoolboy who cannot remember his sums may not have any difficulty with who played who at soccer – even who scored the goals!

The same is true with regard to recall. We can recall easiest the things which we have found interesting. An interest in something leads us to pay attention. Paying attention also involves us concentrating a little harder than usual. Both attention and concentration allow the information to pass from short-term memory and into long-term memory. In other words, they increase the likelihood of retention. Attention and concentration also improve a person's recall of information. This is best illustrated in the idea of the 'absent-minded professor'. The professor does not have a poor memory (certainly not for his own subject), he simply pays little attention to everyday things.

Most people's main problem is not with memory as such, but rather with the recall of information. Even when the information is definitely retained, there can still be a problem of recalling it into conscious awareness. Recall partly depends on how the information was stored in the brain in the first place. For instance, was it achieved by means of a picture, was it linked to something that you already knew, etc? We have already noted that if something is unusual or outstanding then it will be remembered (recalled). Studies also indicate that we tend to remember more about the first (primacy) and last (recency) items or events more than those in the middle. This is why when giving a lecture, talk or writing, it is useful to say what you intend to cover, cover the material, and then indicate the important points you have covered. Recall is also improved if the information is linked to something – preferably something itself unusual or to something that you already know very well. The reason for this is fairly obvious. To say that you know something very well means (amongst other things) that you can readily recall it to your consciousness. So, whatever you link to this will also be brought up to your consciousness.

One final observation about recall is worth making. Studies indicate that something which is repeated frequently is more likely to be remembered. This seems to aid in the successful coding of information into long-term memory. If, however, this is linked with a relaxed state then not only is the coding more successful, but the recall is also more probable. We notice this most (in its negative form) when we are anxious or nervous. In these circumstances recall seems to be impeded – the name is on the tip of your tongue, but it just alludes you. Frequent relaxation, as given on page 10, or any other method, will have the added advantage that your memory will improve both in terms of retention and in terms of recall.

As we shall see shortly, one of the aims of creative visualization is to increase our attention (and interest) and to concentrate more directly on the information which we are wanting to retain. It is also a means of making useful links between the new information and that already stored in our heads. By doing this not only is retention improved but so is the recall of information.

Creative Visualization and Memory

An image is a mental construction which has been created by the mind without the immediate sense stimulus. If I said, 'Imagine a unicorn', most probably you would picture a (white?) horse with a horn in the centre of its forehead. No such thing, of course, exists, but the image is clear enough for most people. Most people readily form pictures in their mind's eye. Some do not even realize that they do so because they have done so all their lives and never given it any thought. But mental pictures are of tremendous importance – and not only for memory.

Imagery has one important feature over a simple picture of an object. It can be *creative*. You can put together in the one image things which are normally separate. The mind has no great difficulty imagining, that is picturing, a little green martian (which is going to be your own image of a green martian) driving a go-cart and being chased by an overgrown caterpillar! The point about this image is that one of the characters in it does not exist, others would not ever be seen together, while one of the items is exaggerated in size: and yet the mind has no real difficulty creating the image. And why would you remember the image I have just created? The reason is that it is unusual. The fact that it is so unusual means that you pay it attention and concentrate on the image being formed in your mind.

Mental pictures, like the one just given, are at the centre of most memory aids – such as the link and peg systems, which we shall deal with in the next section. But as we observed in the first section of this book, images are features of the right hemisphere of the brain and as such are best recalled if they are:

1 Ridiculous, amusing and/or illogical
2 Out of proportion
3 Carrying out some action
4 Exaggerated in number
5 Substituted for by something else

A perusal of this list will readily reveal that they all occur in dreams (as we outlined in Chapter 2), and this is the very reason why they work. The brain naturally uses these features every night, whether you recall your dreams or not. By utilizing them consciously all you are doing is carrying out something already familiar to the workings of the brain. What it basically does is allow you to remember things not only by attempting to do so with the left hemisphere of the brain, but by invoking both hemispheres. It would appear that the right hemisphere is better at imagery than the left, but it requires a different process than that which the left normally uses.

Let us briefly go through the list. You pay attention to something which is out of the ordinary. To remember something, therefore, you create a picture of it in some ridiculous or illogical situation. Most important, be creative in the picture that you form. Take something simple like 'carpet'.

It is no good picturing a carpet in your living room. This is too familiar and will not readily come to mind. Rather, imagine seeing a flying carpet (as in the *Arabian Nights*) come shooting down from the sky at high speed and land directly at your feet.

Seeing objects out of proportion is an excellent memory aid. Do not simply double them in size. Increase their size tenfold, or even larger. Suppose, for example, you had to remember 'stethoscope'. Do not picture a doctor with a stethoscope listening to someone's chest. Again, this is too ordinary and will not imprint itself clearly on your memory. If, on the contrary, you pictured an enormous stethoscope with its central section right up to an enormous pumping heart then, I think, you would have little difficulty remembering 'stethoscope'. Notice also in this picture the illogicality – the stethoscope directly listening to the heart rather than a person's chest. This illustrates what has been referred to as a 'logical illogical association'.

The mind seems to remember things best when they involve action and movement. This can be most useful when you require to remember a sequence of things where the order matters. The action involves the objects or things appearing in the correct sequence. Suppose you wish to remember: carpet, stethoscope and banana. These are a totally independent list of objects and this is why remembering them causes difficulties. Of course, the list is small, but it is the principle that is being dealt with here. You should have no difficulty even now remembering the image for 'carpet' and the image for 'stethoscope'. You now form a composite picture which is all action. You see, in your mind's eye, the flying carpet come swooping down from the sky at top speed. It comes right through the window and comes to rest just by an enormous pumping heart with an enormous stethoscope listening to it. The heart then turns into a large banana which begins to unfold its skin like an enormous flower. The sequence is established by the action. Although the image takes some time to put down in words, it forms in the mind in a flash with no difficulty at all. Once formed the sequence can be read – forwards and backwards.

Exaggerating the number of items can also be an aid to memory. Again take the list of three: carpet, stethoscope and banana. Have the scene unfold as before, but now in the last part of the action see the heart turn into a shower of bananas which rise up and then fall to the ground. Make sure there are hundreds of them. It is the exaggeration that imprints the image on your mind.

Finally, there is the act of substitution; e.g. a saucepan replacing a hat, a sausage replacing a pen, or one suggested to you by someone else. Imagery is a very subjective and personal activity. No two people will throw up the same image in response to a given word. Since it is your memory which is being improved it is your images which will aid the process. But image formation, like those just outlined, require some practice. The reason is that we do not engage very frequently in such activity at the waking level. Once, however, you get the idea of forming images then they soon readily spring to mind.

Such images are excellent for remembering someone's name. The image not only includes objects which reveal the name, but it can also include items that highlight some characteristic about the person, such as their job. Suppose you are introduced to June Simpson, a school teacher. On being introduced you should try to create in your mind's eye some composite picture which incorporates all relevant information. You may, for instance, have a picture of a half moon with '6' in the crest ('moon' sounding like June and '6' being an added reminder that it is the sixth month). This falls down and into a sink with a young boy in it and his mother saying that she will tell teacher about his misbehaviour. Here, the contrived link is between sink (for simp) and son. Notice that in this scene the occupation comes from the speech. Recollection of speech can often be remembered quite easily (see Chapter 1) and is an added aid to the scene. Again, the scene took far longer to describe than to create in the mind's eye.

Peg and Link Systems of Memory

The peg and link systems of memory are based very much on the creative visualization which we outlined in the previous section. These two systems are by far the most popular and most effective of all memory aid systems. This should not be surprising considering that they utilize the characteristics of the right hemisphere of the brain, and it is this hemisphere which seems best suited to memory improvement. It is not our intention to give the systems in detail, since these have been dealt with elsewhere. The essentials of the systems, however, are quite straightforward. We shall first describe the link system and then the peg system.

The link system

This is used for remembering a string of objects, names, etc. We shall again keep the list short and use the three: carpet, stethoscope and banana. The idea is to begin by linking the first word to something you do know. You then link this, by means of a pictorial image, with the next. Having established this association, you then take the next object and link this with the previous one. In doing this you always link the new object with one that you know, i.e. have just learnt. The process is shown in the following schema:

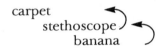

carpet
   stethoscope
     banana

You may for instance imagine your own living room carpet being unrolled in front of you. Inside are hundreds of stethoscopes which all land at your feet. Having crystallized this image you then turn to the next object; namely the banana. The aim now is to create another image which links the banana with a stethoscope. You could imagine an operating theatre with a large banana lying on the operating table and the doctor 'listening' to its heart.

The essence of this system is that the link is a strong one and always links the unknown with the known. Although each image is separate, the links soon bring them to mind. They come to mind most clearly if they conform to the list given in the previous section, i.e. if they are (1) ridiculous, amusing and/or illogical, (2) out of proportion, (3) involve action, (4) are exaggerated in number, and (5) involve substitution.

Peg system

The peg system is a little more sophisticated but has tremendous application and potential. It is based on ten sounds (and is therefore a phonetic system). These sounds are based on consonants only and no vowels are involved. These ten sounds represent the numbers 1, 2, . . ., 9, 0. The ten sounds are:

1	T, D	6	J, Sh, Ch, g (soft)
2	N	7	K, C (hard), g (hard)
3	M	8	F, V
4	R	9	B, P
5	L	0	Z, S

These sound must be memorized along with the numbers that they are associated with.

Having learnt these sounds the next step is to create ten words involving just each one of these sounds. The words themselves should be simple, but preferably things that you can picture. Although you could create your own list, here is the first ten most commonly used:

1	Tie	6	Shoe
2	Noah	7	Key
3	Ma	8	Ivy
4	Ray	9	Bee
5	Law	10	Toes

Notice that we created 10 form two sounds: T for 1 and S for 0, hence *Toes* can be nothing other than 10. In the same way any number can be created with its associated phonetic word. For instance, 16 is *Dish*: D for 1 and Sh for 6. Clearly, once the idea is understood you can immediately deduce the number from the word. For example, *Rain* is composed of two sounds, R and N, and it must therefore represent the number 42.

The list of words must be rote learned, but since they conform to a phonetic pattern it is easier to learn this, say, hundred than an arbitrary list of one hundred objects. Since the list must be learned, and once learned remains fixed, there is the problem of doing this. One procedure is to learn them in groups of twenty-five. On page 114 I provide a computer program to help this process along. If you do not have a computer you will find the list of 100 words at the end of the program.

Up to this point no creative visualization is involved. But it should have already crossed your mind what the next step is. Whenever you have a list of objects, names, etc., to remember then you peg them to the list. Thus our list (carpet, stethoscope and banana) would be pegged to the first three objects (Tie, Noah and Ma). Following the procedures of creative visualization already outlined, you may imagine, for instance, a man trying to put on a carpet for a tie and getting himself in a complicated mess. You will then imagine two stethoscopes going into Noah's ark. Finally, you could imagine Ma hitting a naughty boy with a banana. Each created visualization is separate but because it is pegged to an already known object there is no difficulty bringing both back into consciousness.

The advantage of this system over the link one is that you can indicate the objects in any order. If I suddenly asked you for the second, you would immediately be thinking of Noah, and it is but a small step to see the two stethoscopes going into the ark. So long as the original image is clear and stands out then you will have no difficulty remembering it.

The peg and link systems can themselves be combined. You may remember that we considered the sequence of numbers 1357246. Now consider this sequence as 13 57 24 6. The peg words associated with each of these numbers are *Tomb, Log, Nero,* and *Shoe.* The procedure now is to link these peg words. You could imagine going down into an Egyptian tomb and opening up the sarcophagus only to find a log of wood in place of a mummy (this could be a confusing image because 'mummy' stands for the number 33). You then picture Nero playing a log in place of his fiddle while Rome is burning away in the background (notice here our first example of substitution – the log in place of the fiddle). Finally, you imagine Nero playing and a host of shoes dancing to the music. Although these take some time to describe in words, the images form very quickly in the mind. Your memory will work better the more imaginative and the more creative you are in your visualization.

Mental Maps as Aids to Memory

Mental maps have been highlighted particularly by Tony Buzan and discussed further by P. Russell, both books of whom are listed in the references. First, what are 'mental maps'? These are constructions, on a piece of paper, which begin with an idea (or point) which is placed in the *centre* of the

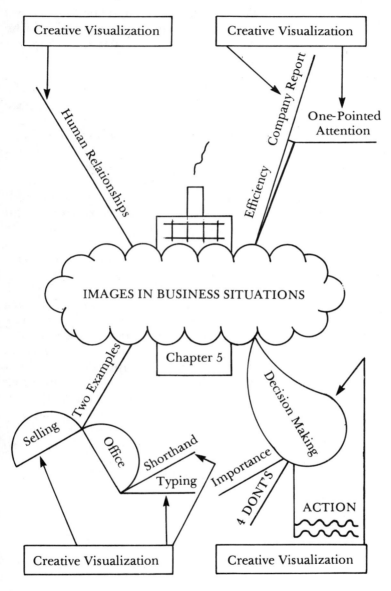

Figure 6

page and then all related ideas are patterned onto this by lines, shapes, colours, etc. Most important is that related aspects are written *along the lines*. It is probably easier to follow the discussion if you first look at a typical mental map. In Figure 6 we have a mental map for Chapter 5, which I used in writing this book.

Why are such maps so useful? To begin with they do not follow a linear fashion: they do not begin at the top of the page and go down the page line by line. Although this has its uses, it is not typical of the way the mind works. As we have pointed out, the mind is holistic and works with patterns and inter-relationships. The mental map utilizes just these principles in setting out information. Because the information is set out in a non-linear fashion, and follows principles about connected-ness, nested ideas, etc. it is more readily accepted by the right hemisphere of the brain. This should not be surprising. The brain does not record and process information in a linear fashion because this is inefficient. The brain looks for patterns, connections, relationships, etc. There is overwhelming evidence that this is true. Suppose, then, that it is true. Now ask yourself, 'Will I remember something better if I present it in a logical linear fashion or in the form of a connected map?' The logical linear presentation of information does have its use, but it appeals only to the left hemisphere of the brain. A mental map, as portrayed in Figure 6, appeals to the right hemisphere of the brain. But we have pointed out that memory seems more related to the right than to the left hemisphere of the brain. It follows, therefore, that any procedure that utilizes right brain processes will be more likely to improve memory. This is why mental maps are so successful and useful.

Mental maps are characterized by:

1 Organization
2 Key words
3 Association
4 Clustering
5 Outstandingness
6 Conscious involvement

All these are features of creative visualization. Even such an obvious and simple aspect as 'key words' can be creative if these are written in capitals, placed in boxes or some outstanding shape and done in a bright colour. When constructing such a mental map you do not merely see what you read, but you observe what you read. Only by observing can you relate the information to that of earlier ideas that are presently on the map. You organize the information as you process it. You highlight immediately the important from the unimportant. You immediately make connections between related ideas – which are far easier than when the information is written on lines on a page. You ignore all irrelevant words and phrases and concentrate only on the essentials. In effect, you construct something on paper which probably comes very close to the way the brain itself processes information. Because of this, the brain more readily absorbs the information contained in a mental map (scientists would say that the two interface).

The most obvious feature of the mental map is that it can be pictured in the mind's eye. The very fact that you have made a picture of the information means that the mind can more readily recall. Each mental map is unique. Since I came across the idea of these maps, I have made hundreds. None of them are the same. They grow and extend themselves as more and more information is acquired. They can readily be added to at different points in time; and, more importantly, they can be pictured with just one look. This means that revision, if it is at all necessary, can be done with almost one look at the map. Whole books can be contained on just one sheet of paper (or a few at the very least). Articles, talks, seminars, etc. can be constructed while you are reading or listening. Problems can be laid out in terms of such maps, and so aid in seeing a possible (and 'best') solution.

As an aid to memory they are invaluable. The very act of constructing them brings to bear your attention and concentration, two features we stressed at the beginning. The maps help in the process of transferring the information from short- to long-term memory, i.e. it helps in achieving a successful coding rather than an unsuccessful one (see Figure 5). Not only does it help in retention, but it also eases recall. This is most likely because the links made on the mental map are similar, if not the same, as those made by the brain. The more we make associations the easier it is to recall information. It is isolated and unconnected pieces of information that we have the most difficulty in remembering.

Conclusion

Although this chapter has concentrated on memory, it is clear that the ideas contained in it apply to many situations. A good memory can aid in decision-making, taking notes, and preparing speeches. Although the uses are manifold, the basic ideas underlying them are the same as all the other aspects of creative visualization that we have been developing in this book. It is this commonality which we are attempting to highlight: we wish to see the wood as well as the trees.

Computer Program

Here we present a computerized version of the Peg System. If you do not have a computer and just wish for the list of 100 words, you will find these on lines 1000-1090 of the program.

This is an interactive program and you do not need to know anything about computer programming. It is in two forms. One is where the computer will ask you to choose the correct word associated with a number. The number itself is chosen at random. If you wish to learn only the first 25, say, then when asked 'The number of peg words' you simply type in 25. If you wish all 100 then you type in 100. Once the number of peg words has been fed in, then the random numbers will be chosen from this set only.

The second form is where the computer gives you the word and you must choose the correct number associated with this word. Again, the word is chosen at random from the collection of words which you specify when you insert the number of peg words.

In both cases you have the option of returning to the 'Menu', i.e. the original list of three options. This allows you to end the program by choosing option 3.

The program itself is written in simple BASIC and should run on most microcomputers. If, however, you do not have a READ/DATA option then this can be overcome by using an INPUT statement and inputting the 100 words at the beginning. The remainder of the program is unaltered.

Computer program

```
100    REM PEG SYSTEM OF REMEMBERING
110    REM WRITTEN BY R SHONE
120    REM MAXIMUM WORD LENGTH SET AT 100
130    CLEAR 500
140    DIM A$ (100)
150    CLS:PRINT"PHONETIC PEG SYSTEM":PRINT
160    PRINT"YOU HAVE THREE OPTIONS:":PRINT
170    PRINT"        1) CHOOSING A WORD ASSOCIATED
       WITH A GIVEN NUMBER"
180    PRINT"        2) CHOOSING A NUMBER
       ASSOCIATED WITH A GIVEN WORD"
190    PRINT"        3) END":PRINT
200    INPUT "THE NUMBER OF PEG WORDS";N
210    INPUT "WHAT IS YOUR CHOICE <1>, <2> OR
       <3>";C
220    ON C GOTO 230, 500, 600
230    FOR I=1 TO N:READ A$(I):NEXT I
240    REM CHOOSING WORD ASSOCIATED WITH A
       GIVEN NUMBER
250    GOSUB 900
260    PRINT"GUESS WORD ASSOCIATED WITH THE
       NUMBER";R:PRINT
270    PRINT"IF WANTING TO RETURN TO MENU,
       INPUT <MENU>"
280    INPUT G$
290    IF G$="MENU" THEN 150
300    IF G$<>B$ THEN 320
310    PRINT"CORRECT":GOTO 250
320    PRINT"NO. TRY AGAIN":GOTO 260
330    REM CHOOSING NUMBER ASSOCIATED WITH
       A GIVEN WORD
500    CLS
510    GOSUB 900
520    PRINT "GUESS THE NUMBER ASSOCIATED
       WITH THE WORD";B$:PRINT
530    PRINT "IF WANTING TO RETURN TO MENU,
       INPUT <0>"
540    INPUT G
```

```
550     IF G=0 THEN 150
560     IF G<>R THEN 580
570     PRINT "CORRECT":GOTO 510
580     PRINT "NO. TRY AGAIN": GOTO 520
600     END
900     REM SUBROUTINE FOR RANDOM NUMBER
        AND ASSOCIATED PEG WORD
910     R = RND(N)
920     B$=A$(R)
930     RETURN
1000    DATA "TIE", "NOAH", "MA", "RAY", "LAW",
        "SHOE", "KEY", "IVY", "BEE", "TOES"
1010    DATA "TIT", "TIN", "TOMB", "TYRE", "TOWEL",
        "DISH", "DOG", "DIVE", "TUB", "NOSE"
1020    DATA "NUT", "NUN", "GNOME", "NERO", "NILE",
        "NUDGE", "NECK", "KNIFE", "NIB", "MOUSE"
1030    DATA "MAT", "MOON", "MUMMY", "MAYOR",
        "MULE", "MATCH", "MUG", "MUFF", "MOB",
        "ROSE"
1040    DATA "RAT", "RAIN", "RUM", "ROAR", "ROLL",
        "RICH", "RACK", "ROOF", "ROBE", "LACE"
1050    DATA "READ", "LION", "LAMB", "LAIR", "LOLLY",
        "LEACH", "LOG", "LOAF", "LIP", "CHEESE"
1060    DATA "SHEET", "CHIN", "JAM", "JAR", "JAIL",
        "CHICHI", "CHALK", "CHIEF", "SHIP", "CASE"
1070    DATA "CAT", "COIN", "COMB", "CARE", "COAL",
        "COSH", "CAKE", "CAVE", "COB", "VASE"
1080    DATA "FAT", "FAN", "VIM", "FIRE", "FILE",
        "FISH", "FOG", "FIFE", "FIB", "BUS"
1090    DATA "BAT", "BONE", "BOMB", "BAR", "BALL",
        "BEACH", "BOOK", "PUFF", "PIPE", "THESIS"
```

9
GOAL-DIRECTED VISUALIZATION

This chapter is basically about being successful: whether successful in the home, in the office, at an interview, at a social gathering, or whatever. It has long been realized that success means achievement, but to achieve something already implies that that something is well defined: that there is a goal and that this goal is well defined. If a goal is not well defined then you never know whether you have achieved it or not. In the first section, therefore, we take up this point about the importance of having well defined goals. But even far away goals, which on the face of it may appear unrealistic, are only so in the short term. In other words, what is important is the time span placed on goals. Big goals can be achieved in a series of well defined steps, each step having a well defined sub-goal. This naturally takes us into the second section where we discuss the importance of plans which must be clearly laid out as to the means of achieving our goals. Clearly, it is no good saying that you wish to become the Prime Minister or President, and then sit back and just hope it will happen. No. We all realize that we must make an effort in achieving our goals; and effort, if it is not to be wasted, must involve a plan of action.

There has been much written on these two aspects; realistic goals and plans of action for achieving such goals. But one feature has been underrated in these two processes; namely, the use of creative visualization. It is possible to define goals in words and to write out plans of action, again in words. But if the whole procedure is to be successful, or more efficient, then utilizing creative visualization is both desirable and necessary. It is necessary because only by using creative visualization will a person involve their subconscious mind fully in the procedure. In this chapter we indicate two ways to take advantage of creative visualization in the specifying of goals and the plans for achieving such goals. This is followed by a simple suggestion of drawing your success and the stages to it. Once again this employs the right hemisphere of the brain and so more readily involves subconscious processes in the task.

A great deal of nonsense has been written about the will, and especially the relationship between imagination and the will. All the same, there is a great deal of truth in the adage that if the will and the imagination are in conflict then it is the imagination that will win out. It is also recognized that the will to succeed is a great force in actually succeeding. In the final section, therefore, we discuss the role of the will in goal-directed visualization, making the point that the will must be properly used in the process if it is not to hinder it in any way. Only by investigating the role of the will can we ascertain how to use the will to best advantage.

Well-Defined and Realistic Goals

A number of people find that they go through life with no clear purpose. They envy those who do seem to have a purpose, thinking that this purpose comes from 'outside' the individual. *All people who have a purpose have made a decision to have one.* It comes not from 'outside' but rather from 'inside' the person. To have a purpose is to have a goal. It may be to be successful, it could be to be rich, it could simply be to be the best darts player in the local. Whatever it is, the goal directs behaviour; it gives the person a reason for the things that they do, and generally it makes them feel happier. In brief, a person who has a goal is a happier person.

Simply stating that having goals makes a person happy is not sufficient. There is a proper way of setting goals and there is an incorrect way of setting goals. In this section we are concerned about the way to set goals correctly so that we get the full benefit of goal-directed visualization.

It will be useful from the outset to list the ten characteristics which goals must have. These are:

1 They must be clear and well defined
2 They must be realistic
3 They must be available
4 They must be based on correct information
5 They must be actively set
6 They must be of interest to us
7 They must be constantly kept in mind
8 They must concern us with the future
9 They must mean something to us
10 They must lead to a plan of action

This is a long list. In this section we shall concentrate on just some of them, leaving later sections for the remainder. Some are so obvious that nothing further will be mentioned about them.

Goals must be clear and well defined. This first requirement of goal setting is most important. It is also the one which people fail at most often. It is not sufficient to have some hazy notion of what we may want. Goals direct our behaviour, and if the target is to be reached by the most efficient route, then the target must be clear and well defined. It is not simply enough to say that 'I wish to be successful'. This begs the question, 'Successful in what?' You must be more specific than that. There are two main reasons for being more specific. First, the more specific you are the easier it is to form a plan of action that will achieve your goal. Second, the more specific your goal the easier it will be to picture it. Each of these will be discussed in the next two sections. In terms of our present example of success, you could be more specific by narrowing down the goal to that of being successful at your job. This is clear and well defined. Also, you would immediately have some idea of what 'success' means in the context of your job.

The next point is that the goal must be realistic. If you are presently the errand boy or girl in a large multinational company then it is unrealistic to set a goal of becoming the company president. It is unrealistic to set as a goal the idea of becoming an astronaut, when you have neither the education nor the skill, and could never attain it even in your lifespan. This is wishful thinking, and not the setting of realistic goals. This does not mean that if you are at the bottom of the pyramid then you should not set a long-term goal of heading it. Rather it implies that long-term goals should be approached in small and gradual stages, where each stage has a well-defined and realistic goal. A realistic goal in fact implies that it is one which is presently available. By this we mean that you have the capacity to achieve it or acquire it. If you have never done any science, it is not in your capacity to discover a new protein molecule. Goals must be just further than where you presently are. Once they are achieved then you can expand the 'sphere of availability' (see Ophiel, *The Art and Practice of Getting Material Things Through Creative Visualization*).

Goals must be of interest to us and mean something to us. Both of these give emotional content to the goal. If we are going to achieve our goals then they must interest us; if they interest us then we direct our attention at them and so they are in our consciousness a great deal of the time. The more meaning the goals have to us, the more we want them and the more we want them the more attention we give to them and the more often they are in our consciousness. We see, then, that interest and meaning have the result that we pay attention to the goals we set and keep them frequently in mind. We keep our eyes on the target, as it were.

Goals must be actively set. By this we mean that you must give them a great deal of thought. In doing this you must find out all you can about the goal concerned. Not all goals require detailed information, but some will. You should get in the habit of taking an interest in setting your goals with full information. To take a simple example. Suppose you wish to be a success in your job. What does this mean? One way is to consider people who have already become successful. Find out all about them and what it is that makes them successful. Try to find out what is the most important feature that a successful person has in your kind of job. The more information you gather the more easily you will be able to lay out a plan of action – a point we shall take up in the next section. It is most important that your information is correct. Goals based on incorrect information are unlikely to succeed.

Finally, goals must be concerned with the future and because of this they must involve a plan of action so that such a future goal can be attained. By being set in the future we do not mean the very far future. To be more specific, the goal must be sufficiently well defined so that the period for its achievement is finite. The period itself may be unspecified, so long as the goal itself is sufficiently well defined that when it is achieved this is known. If this is not done, then your behaviour will constantly be driven to achieve this never achievable goal! To be rich, for example, is not a well defined goal. How rich is rich? If you do not specify how rich, then you may spend the rest of your life accumulating riches – even when you have quite sufficient for your needs. You could alternatively set a goal of £x. When is is achieved you can then set another amount – if money is what you want. By doing this you can always stop this particular behaviour by not setting another goal for the accumulation of yet more money.

Setting Plans
Having clearly set your goals, as outlined in the previous section, the next and vital step is to lay out a plan of action for achieving such goals. Too often people set themselves goals and then sit back hoping they will be achieved. This is not the way to achieve successful goals. It is important that you set out a plan of action. This plan itself must be clear and realistic, just in the same way that the goals had to be clear and realistic. If you are the undermanager, you could have a plan of action which involved shooting the manager so that you could take over. Notice that this is definitely a plan of action, and that it is clear and precise. It is, however, unrealistic. A plan involves doing something. What this action is clearly depends on the goal which has been set. We see here the importance of a well-defined goal. If the goal is well defined then this will often indicate the type of action necessary for its achievement. Take a very simple case. Suppose you wish to meet a person of the opposite sex to whom you would like to get attached. It is no good staying in every night. Clearly the plan of action that is called for is to see what changes you must make in your behaviour that are necessary for this goal to be achieved. It may be to go out more frequently. It may be considering in some depth about the places you already go and seeing whether a change in venue is called for where you are more

likely to meet someone of the opposite sex. It may involve you joining some local group where you are likely to meet someone of the opposite sex. Whatever it is, it is clear that it must involve action and it must involve a change in your behaviour: which is the whole basis of a plan. Only by doing this will the goal be feasible. A goal cannot be achieved by doing nothing.

The setting of a plan of action is again a purposeful activity. The person who sets goals and then sets plans for achieving those goals cannot do other than reveal a purposeful behaviour. To others they appear to know what they want and know how to get it. But this is not particular to them. It is because they have chosen to be this way. They know that by setting goals and the means of achieving those goals that they do achieve them; and because they achieve them they then set other goals and actions for achieving these in turn. Such behaviour is repeated throughout their lives. In doing this they are happy because they have purpose. Each day they get up they know what they must do because they have a well-defined plan of action. Until the goal is achieved the action must be modified and corrected.

This immediately brings us to another feature of plans of action. A plan of action must be flexible enough to allow for detours. The quickest way between two houses in a city is how the crow flies. Unless you are going to climb over buildings, this is clearly not the most sensible and quickest route for a human being to take. The action involves first deciding whether you are going to walk, take a bus or tram, or go by car or taxi. Each of these are feasible, realistic and will achieve the stated target (goal). Once this decision is made then others naturally follow. Suppose you are familiar with the city and you intend to walk. You begin by taking your usual route. But you now find that one road you usually take is blocked off for road-works. You re-route to take account of this obstruction. You change (or correct) your plan of action in the process of carrying it out. This is true of goals involving your future. When faced with some unforeseen obstruction your plan must be flexible enough for some change to be made. You must realize that there will always occur some setbacks in the achievement of goals. These should not be considered disastrous, rather they should be treated as mere obstructions which call for a change in behaviour in order to avoid them.

A plan of action for the achievement of a goal may itself involve a series of minor goals. These minor goals may be natural stages on the way to achieving the major goal. Suppose, for instance, that you wished to be the managing director, but you have only just joined the company as a trainee manager. Your first task, your first minor goal, is to become the manager of your section. You must then set up a plan of action that will eventually achieve this goal. Having achieved this goal, your next stage may be to become the plant manager. This involves a different plan of action. Once this is achieved then you set a goal of becoming area manager; and so on until you achieve your final goal. Each of the subsidiary goals has a natural progression leading to the final goal. Each minor goal is clear and well defined. These combine to define the plan of action to achieve the major goal. This example also illustrates the importance of having a flexible plan of action. Clearly, there are many routes to managing director. As you progress through the minor goals you may have to adapt or re-route to take account of some unforeseen happening – for example, a takeover of the company by a large corporation.

Notice too that plans of action for achieving goals have many of the characteristics that goals themselves have. Not only must the plan of action be clear and well defined, but it must be realistic. The plan must involve a means which is available to you. For instance, the goal may involve some knowledge which you presently do not possess. In this case the plan, if it is to be feasible, must involve you in acquiring such knowledge first. This, too, indicates that a plan of action is based on information about the means for achieving such a goal. In the case of going from one house to another in the same city, for instance, this requires you to know the road system and have information about the buses which will get you in the proximity of where you wish to go. In the case of the undermanager, it involves having knowledge and information about the workings of the company, its personnel, etc. The plan of action must be to your liking. In other words, it must not be against your moral code or involve you in doing things which you think are harmful to other people. This is not the same as doing things you dislike. Part of the aim of setting plans is to change your behaviour pattern, and generally people dislike change. But you have only one choice. If you dislike change then you will not go about setting a plan of action and so no goal can be achieved! The only way that a goal can possibly be achieved is by allowing for change. You must get used to wanting change; and because change often leads to mistakes, you must also get used to making mistakes. But as most educators know, you learn more from your mistakes than from your successes. So you must not get upset by making mistakes, but concentrate on what you can learn from them.

Up to this point we have simply set out the basic ideas about setting goals and setting plans for achieving such goals. No mention has been made so far of creative visualization. The ideas outlined so far have been said many times and in many books, and we have simply summarized them here. But they can be taken further.

So far the account has been very logical and sets out the process in a step-wise fashion. There is nothing wrong with this, and it must be undertaken. But it utilizes only the features of the left hemisphere of the brain. It in no way involves the right hemisphere of the brain. Does this mean that the right hemisphere of the brain has nothing to contribute to the setting of goals and the plans for their achievement? The answer is, 'No'. The right hemisphere has quite a lot to contribute to this process. In the next two sections we shall discuss two ways in which the right hemisphere can be used to contribute to the process of setting goals and plans for achieving them. The first is actually visualizing, in your mind's eye, the goals and the plans. The second is drawing your goals and plans.

Visualizing Your Goals and Plans of Action

Goals can be creatively visualized. Although plans can also be creatively visualized, it is more difficult to do so than visualizing goals. Furthermore, it is more important to visualize goals than it is to visualize plans.

We have repeatedly made the point that goals must be clear and well defined. Part of the reason for this is so that you can visualize quite clearly your goal. Success, as a goal, is simply too vague. To visualize success, you would have to be more specific as to what you mean by success. If it is success at your job, even this is too vague. What does it mean to be successful at your job? Let us suppose that it means becoming local plant manager, shop steward, local branch chairperson, or whatever. The art of creative visualization is to now picture yourself, in your mind's eye, being *that* person. It is not simply a question of seeing in your mind's eye the present person and wishing you were in their shoes. This is wishful thinking and not creative visualization. What you must do is be in that job which you have designated as success. You must imagine you already have the position, you must visualize your actions, behaviour and relationships with other people. In other words, you must become that success in your mind's eye. You must see it, feel it, and become it, in every way possible.

What is the best way to carry out this creative visualization? It is possible to close your eyes and visualize it, especially when on some journey. But this is inefficient. Goal-directed visualization is a creative process. You are likely to arrive at a clearer and well-defined image of your goal if you get into a relaxed state, as outlined on page 10. Once relaxed you can then let the goal formulate itself, with some prodding, in your mind's eye. By doing this you are using the right hemisphere of the brain more effectively. Your mind will likely throw up an image of your success, which on the face of it might not seem like an image of success. But you will know that it feels right. The point about this is that the brain is giving rise to an image, just as in dreams, which has emotional content and has meaning to your particular psyche. Even if you have defined success as a particular position, as we indicated above, your subconscious mind when in this relaxed state will enable you to visualize positions and situations that you would be dealing with if you had such a post. By doing this you will obtain knowledge of what it feels like being in such a position. One of the features of creative visualization is to allow you to have emotional involvement, emotional commitment, to your goal.

Take another simple example. Suppose your goal is to have x amount of money. The first thing that should come to mind is that, in itself, this is not a well-defined goal. Only for the miser or Scrooge is the goal well-defined – only for them is the accumulation of money an end in itself. But for most people the point of having a goal like this is so that you can obtain something that you want. This is very important. In our list of ten characteristics which goals must possess, two of them show that they must be of interest to you and that they must mean something to you. This example, therefore, illustrates the point of clearly specifying your major goal. Suppose it is having enough money to buy your own home. The major goal is owning your own home, rather than having x amount of money. Two courses of action are open to you at this point. First, you can simply visualize owning your own home in as much detail as you can. How you get it is left undefined. Alternatively, you can set a subsidiary goal of accumulating the money to buy your own home. This requires a plan of action which allows you to obtain money. It is not sufficient to sit back and hope that you will win on the pools or that some unknown rich uncle or aunt will leave you a fortune. Obviously, then, you will need to decide on some means of getting money. One possibility is doing extra work on the side – either related to your job or with respect to some hobby you may have. Let us suppose that you have now decided on a course of action that will bring in some money. Even if the money is only a small amount at a time, that does not matter. What you do then is, while in a relaxed state, visualize yourself carrying out this extra work. See it, feel it, and be it in every way. See in particular your bank balance rising as each extra job brings in more and more money. Include in your visualization more and more success. In other words, initially visualize yourself being asked to do various jobs. Then visualize being given some special jobs which bring in even more money because of their responsibility. Visualize people at your door asking, pleading for you to do a job for them, that if you only would they would pay you very handsomely. As each new job arrives and your money begins to accumulate, keep your major goal constantly in mind. Visualize your bank balance rising and you going out and buying your new home. Visualize the whole process and, equally important, let yourself feel the elation of having achieved your goal by your own efforts.

By visualizing your goals and your plans for achieving such

goals while in a relaxed state, the images will be more vivid and you will find your own subconscious mind throwing up images which will appeal to you and aid you in the process. What you will find, however, is that once these images are well formulated you will be able to see them, in your mind's eye, very easily at any time of the day (or night), most particularly when walking along the road or in the park, while on the bus or driving along in a car – and it is important that you do do so. As we pointed out, goals must be constantly kept in mind.

Drawing Your Goals and Plans

In this section I wish to develop a procedure which combines the mental maps we have already discussed in the previous chapter and what Ophiel, in his *The Art and Practice of Getting Material Things Through Creative Visualization*, calls Treasure charts. Let me first simply describe the procedure without comment, after which we can consider some points about making and using such drawings.

Basically the aim is to draw your goal and the plan of action that will lead up to it – including any alternative routes that may occur to you. The drawing will be organic, in the sense that you will construct it over an interval of time and the shape it takes will depend on how the future turns out, and how you may have to alter or correct your plan as circumstances change. You begin with a large blank piece of paper – the larger the better, but a plain sheet of A4 paper will do. You first draw a border all around the piece of paper. This is a symbolic representation of a definite goal with a finite time for achieving it. In addition, the border is a symbolic representation of the things which are available to you at the present time, or that you will acquire in the near future in order to achieve your goal. Your present position is located at the *bottom* of the page in the centre, while the goal to be achieved is placed at the *top* of the page and in the centre. The goal should be a brief statement enclosed in some shape which stands out; colour it if necessary. To help you see the process in action, Figure 7 provides such a chart.

This chart is the author's 'goal-directed visualization for the publication of a book on *Creative Visualization*'. It begins with an idea, which once formed leads to the goal of having a book

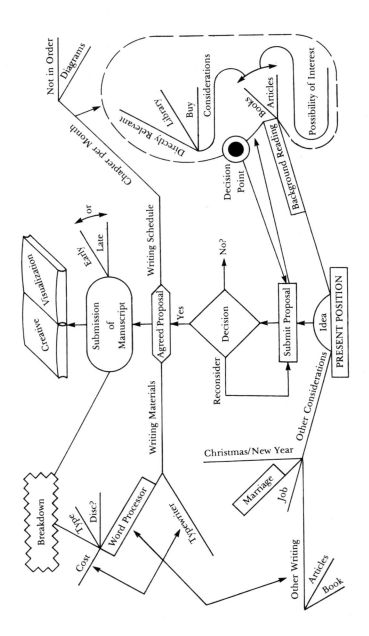

Figure 7

published. There is a natural plan of action, which runs up the centre of the chart. In order to submit even a proposal, some knowledge of the area is required. A prerequisite, therefore, is background reading. This not only supplies knowledge about the subject, but it also provides information on other works of a similar nature. At some point in time, a decision is made to write up a proposal. While a decision is being made on the proposal further reading and research is undertaken. It is rare in publishing to have the first proposal accepted without any change, and so any comments from the publisher will lead to further reading and the submission of a second proposal. Once this is agreed then the writing starts in earnest.

Even here a writing schedule is necessary, not only so you can see if you are on target as regards the time horizon, but also because each chapter can be treated as a minor subgoal in its own right. The writing, of course, requires continued reading and research. But there is also the practical consideration about the method of writing. It is possible to write it long hand and then have it professionally typed; it is possible to type it oneself. In my case I had already decided on the use of modern technology and intended to use a word processor. (The reason for this is because I do a great deal of writing with regard to my job and so the word processor could increase efficiency with regard to all my writing.) But this decision itself led to a slight detour. I had first to master my Superscripsit word processor package, and then I had to transfer onto this what I had already typed on the simpler Scripsit package.

Other commitments (constraints) had constantly to be kept in mind, since they may have required a change in direction of the plan. For instance, during the writing of this book I was also committed to writing another book with respect to my job. In addition, I had planned to get married approximately half way through the time horizon I had set for the achievement of the goal. With all these laid down on the map, I could see everything in perspective with no difficulty. Throughout the period of the plan the goal was constantly kept in mind.

The maps that are constructed can be changed and added to over time. If, for instance, the publishers had rejected the proposal (and assuming they had given a reason) then a new course of action would have been called for. The point about such maps is that you can look at them from time to time, ponder over them and let the whole idea sink into your consciousness. This is more likely with such a map because the whole plan and the goal can be seen 'at a glance'. This wholeness is something which appeals to the right hemisphere of the brain, while the obvious time sequence of events in the plan appeals to the left hemisphere of the brain. Both hemispheres of the brain are actively participating in the whole process.

Imagination and the Will

The will is not only a slippery concept but it is also misunderstood – largely because people confuse 'will' with the effort of holding back, i.e. with 'willpower'. This Victorian idea of will is that it is a negative force leading to restraint. This is a misconception of the function of the will. The function of the will is to direct and not to impose (see Assagioli (1974) and Ferrucci (1982)). In its function of direction it is involved in decisions. If you decide to raise your arm you must invoke the will to achieve this goal. In achieving any goal the will plays a part. The will is like an orchestra leader. He does not himself play, but he directs the overall performance: he sets the direction and tempo of the music; he gives it interpretation and emphasis. So, too, with the will.

Because the will gives purpose and direction it comes very much into play during the plan, rather than in the goal itself. You can, of course, use the will incorrectly. You can steer a sailing boat into the wind or you can use the wind to sail the boat. Using the will incorrectly is like sailing into the wind. The task at hand is not necessarily impossible, but it is more difficult than it need be.

The construction of the maps outlined in the previous section will enable you to use the will to aid the imagination and not try to oppose it. The very act of making the map sets up the 'right' relationship between the will and the imagination.

10
IMAGERY IN RELIEVING PAIN AND REGAINING HEALTH

The resurgence of interest in the mind-body problem has led to a more widely held belief that the mind can affect the body– for better or for worse. The basic principle of holistic medicine is that your mind and body are inseparable. Treating the body as if it is separate from the mind is not really a cure; the whole person must be treated – mind and body. Another principle of holistic medicine is that preventive medicine is important. The dependence on drugs especially treats the illness very passively. When you are ill you take a pill and hope for a cure. It may occur – and not always because of the pill, but more because of your belief in the efficacy of such a pill. You have no conscious participation in this process of curing. Holistic medicine, however, is by no means passive. You are expected to participate consciously in the healing process. Whether you are taking drugs or not, holistic medicine is based on marshalling the body's own healing mechanisms and con- sciously bringing them to bear on the problem.

In this chapter we shall discuss how this can be done. It is not intended that you do not see a doctor. Using your imagination is hardly likely to heal a broken bone! Holistic medicine is supportive in that you participate *with* the doctor in the healing process. If the illness is brought about by the mind then it is possible to heal without the doctor's aid. But in this regard you would need to know a great deal about your mind and about your illness.

Belief plays a very important role in the process of cure. It is important that you believe that you can cure yourself, or help in curing yourself. If you are a sceptic then there are only two courses open to you: ignore it or have a try with as open a mind as possible. In addition, it is important to have more than one attempt. You are involved in learning something new. You cannot expect to be an expert on the first attempt!

Pain is common to many illnesses. We know quite a lot about what pain is not, but not a great deal about what pain actually is. It is not the case that pain is associated with a particular nerve fibre, which when it becomes excited is registered in the brain as pain. Although this is true of senses like sight and sound, it is not the case for pain. But this does give us a clue because it does mean that pain is not so much associated with the spine or the periphery of the nervous system, but rather with the brain itself. It appears that pain has something to do with the imbalance arising from a pattern of nerve impulses. This pattern arises from the fact that there are three pathways through the spine to the brain, as we shall see; it is likely that pain is created by all three.

Man seeks out stimulation and when body signals indicate damage of any kind we feel pain. Man, like other organisms, has programmed within itself a mechanism of withdrawal whenever such pain is registered. It is clear that this mechanism of withdrawal is vital if an organism is going to survive. What we do know is that signals that are registering pain, do in fact get referred to the reward centres of the core brain. But pain is formless and has no cortical representation. By this we mean that there is no area of the cortex specifically designated for pain, as there are for various other parts of the body and motor areas for movement. Put simply and pictorially, the body and all its functions are mapped out onto the cortex, with greater areas for the more functionally important parts. But pain does not appear on this map!

Pain is not simply the absence or opposite of pleasure, since masochists find pain pleasurable! Nor does it seem to be the case that the body maximises pleasure or minimises pain. Until we know more about pain, we cannot be sure what is being undertaken. But we do know some subjective observations about pain. Certainly it cannot be shared. In addition, it depends on social situations; in particular past experiences and the culture to which the person belongs.

Pain can be caused by physiological and emotional factors. The fact that pain can and does vary with our state of mind makes it very difficult to make generalized statements about it. Awareness of pain depends on whether we pay it any attention; e.g. the 'disappearance' of mild pain when we are watching an absorbing film. If we are depressed pain is worse than if we are emotionally elated. What appears to be the case is that the pain *threshold* tends to depend on physiological factors while the *tolerance* to pain tends to depend on psychological factors. One interesting aspect of this is 'body language', such as 'I'm carrying a load on my back' which may lead to lower back pain, or 'People get under my skin'. (An interesting discussion of body language is in Lowen's *Bioenergetics*, Chapter III.) Although we may ignore pain temporarily as we direct our attention elsewhere, awareness inevitably returns. No matter how much pain we feel, we do not become habituated with regard to it, as we do for example with a repetitive sound.

From these comments it is apparent that pain is at the heart of the mind-body problem. It seems to incorporate the whole nervous system and has something to do with the relationship between mind and body, and so has no cortical representation.

The format of this chapter, therefore, is a discussion of the anatomy of pain, followed by a creative visualization method for dealing with pain. We then present a further creative visualization method for dealing with illness in general. This is followed by a more general discussion about forming your own images. A now popular technique of creative visualization is the use of the TV screen, and this is also discussed. A more unusual technique of creative visualization, which I have called the 'Inner-Body Search', follows. Although a long chapter, there are a number of creative visualization techniques which can be used – not only in the case of illness, but also in the many other uses we have discussed in this book.

The Anatomy of Pain

Let us use a simple illustration to discuss some features of pain, namely putting your finger over a candle flame, as drawn in Figure 8.

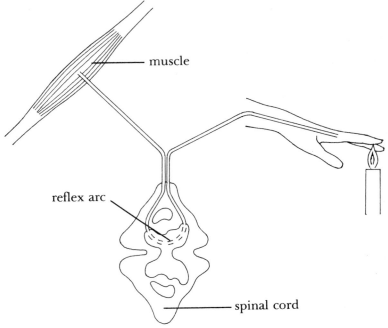

Figure 8

First, nerve endings in the tip of the finger pick up a sensation which leads to a nerve impulse being sent along the nerves. Initially it by-passes the brain by means of the reflex arc in the spinal cord, which immediately relays a message to the muscles to initiate pulling the arm away for protection. Then a nerve impulse is sent up to the brain. Nerves fall into three categories, which are labelled 'A', 'B' and 'C'. Nerve type 'A' is a thick nerve and conducts nerve impulses quickly. Nerve type 'C' is a thin nerve and conducts nerve impulses slowly. When the finger is initially pulled away there is, in the first instance, a sharp localized sensation of pain which arises from impulses passing along 'A' nerves. Then later we feel a dull aching sensation which arises from impulses passing along 'C' nerves. Deep seated pains, which arise from internal organs, tend to be passed along 'C' nerves while pain associated with the periphery of the nervous system tend to arise from a mixture of 'A' and 'C' nerve impulses. (Here we ignore 'B' nerves.)

There are, in fact, three pathways through the spine to the brain, and all three are probably involved in the sensation that we call pain. When the signals arrive in the brain they go to three places. First to the Reticular Activating System (RAS), which in simple terms tells us to do something. This is the basic programming of withdrawal built into all organisms. Second, a message is sent to the cortex of the brain which allows us to establish where the pain is, and also possibly what kind it is. Third, a message goes to the thalamus which evaluates the pain. The situation is shown in Figure 9.

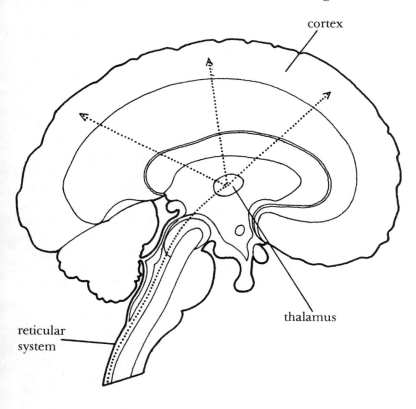

Figure 9

The Reticular Activating System (RAS) not only is involved in pain, but it is also involved in motivation and emotion, along with whole states of the brain – as in sleeping and waking. It is, therefore, worth commenting on it further. As French (1957) puts it:

> without it, an individual is reduced to a helpless, senseless, paralyzed blob of protoplasm.

The reticular formation acts like an alarm clock and awakens the cortex so that it can interpret the incoming sensory signals. The RAS learns to be selective in its sensitivity. A mother can be aroused by the cry of her baby, i.e. the RAS activates her cortex, while in the case of the father no such arousal may occur. Why different people are sensitive to various noises, smells, etc., has probably got something to do with the RAS. It is the RAS which keeps a person conscious (as distinct from asleep) and a damaged RAS can lead to a permanent coma. An alert state, as in hypnosis or altered states of consciousness, seems to depend on the interplay between the cortex and the RAS. This is also true of attention and most likely many other mental processes.

It is not surprising that a number of drugs, e.g. tranquillizers, affect the RAS by blocking the flow of nerve impulses so that the cortex is not activated via this particular route. It appears that the brain (and other parts of the body) can produce its own chemical for abolishing pain, now called *endorphins*. These are contained in the RAS and probably reduce the transmission of signals. This is almost certainly what happens in the case of a pain causing substance, referred to as the *P-factor*, which occurs in the nerve cells. This is all very new and exciting work which will continue to give us new insights into the brain and the mind.

This concludes our brief introduction to the anatomy of pain and anyone interested in looking further could consult Wright *et al* (1970) for a good introduction to the nervous system, Young (1978) for some new researches on the brain, and French (1957) for a straightforward discussion of the RAS. We now turn to the use of imagery and see how this knowledge can help us in using creative visualization to reduce or eliminate pain.

Pain as a Person or Creature

This section draws on the ideas put forward by Simonton *et al* (1978) in their work on cancer. We shall not here be concerned with cancer and pain in terminal illness, but the reader interested in this would do well to consult this work – which is now available in paperback. Their analysis demonstrates that a knowledge of the problem helps in creating visual images of the illness. We have taken up this point in the present chapter which is why we have used the first section to discuss what we know about pain.

In what follows we shall be recounting some specific images. These are purely illustrative and we shall be using them to make some general points about formulating your own. In all cases the first task is to get into a relaxed or hypnotic state, as outlined on page 10. This state in itself will reduce pain to some extent. This arises for two reasons. First, muscle tension is reduced. We pointed out above that muscle contraction (i.e. muscle tension) likely produces a pain-creating substance, the 'P-factor'. Relaxation, therefore, reduces or prevents this eventuality. Second, the relaxation and imagery increases the expectation of success. Expectation of success plays a very vital role. We know already that pain is linked to emotion and if expectation is negative then pain will be harder to overcome. You must have a positive expectation, that is an expectation of success. Believe wholeheartedly in your own body's ability to achieve success.

Let me outline the procedure briefly before going into it in detail. The idea is to imagine your pain as a person or creature. Once you have achieved this you talk to it. You ask it questions, and even ask how you can get rid of it! The point is that the person or creature is simply a creation of your own psyche, your own subconscious mind. It is your right brain operating by means of pictures, as in your dreams. There is nothing magical or supernatural about this. If you conjure up, say, a black panther, then there is nothing strange, at least to the right brain, the subconscious, in endowing this with speech. Walt Disney was a past master at this.

The following deals with a number of sessions over which 'contact' with the pain was made. It is, in fact, my own imagery. Briefly, I had twisted my spine some eight years before, but had not been wholly convinced that the pain was purely physical. It had, I believe, an emotional content with regard to guilt in relation to a change of job. This in itself is very important. Researchers are quite convinced that a number of forms of prolonged pain arise from self-induced punishment. Even when the physical reason for the pain has been removed, it is possible for the pain to continue because the person 'needs' the pain. It is this emotional aspect of the pain that this chapter is directed at overcoming.

> *Session 1*   Pain manifested itself as a big ferocious black cat with enormous sharp teeth pulling at my spine. White birds came and tried to chase the cat away, but it was reluctant to go and kept returning.

In this initial session the aim was simply to create an image of the pain as a person or creature. In this instance a black cat sprung immediately into my mind. Do not choose what the person or creature is to be. It is very important to let the subconscious mind represent it in its own way. In the present illustration the cat is very ferocious. The fact that it is *black* and the teeth are large and pointed indicate anger. It is often the case that associated with pain is anger – anger at yourself, someone else or life in general. The birds being white represent the body's attempt to deal with the pain – probably a representation of the white blood cells. But there is not enough of them and certainly not sufficient to deal with the cat. Also of importance is that as far as the imagery was concerned the cat was clear and dominating the scene. The birds were not very distinct at all. One final observation is that the scene is negative and indicates lack of success. It was at this stage that a conversation with the cat was helpful.

> *Session 2*   Talked with the cat. Asked it, 'What are you here for?' Told that I deserved to be taught a lesson for giving up one job for another (it was, in fact, more specific in its details). I then asked it whether I had not suffered enough. To which he replied, 'Yes.' He went on that now he would not simply go, he had to be driven away. 'Those birds,' he remarked with contempt, 'are too puny.' I then asked him what would drive him away. 'Being eaten alive by

hoards of white cells!' I then 'sent in' a whole swarm of white cells, like a swarm of locusts, which began to devour the cat (where now the cat was completely covered by the cells). The area was then bathed. A number of little men came in with buckets of water which they threw at the area washing away the debris and inflammation.

This was an extremely vivid scene. During it there were emotional signs of relief and on occasions release of tension in the stomach muscles. Notice that the questions were not pre-formulated, they arose from the scene as it unfolded. Here we observe a typical feedback mechanism in operation. Even so, it is important that you ask it questions, such as:

- Why are you here?
- What purpose do you serve?
- Do you have any messages for me?
- How can I get rid of you?

Once the scene begins to unfold the type of questions to ask will become more obvious. Notice how more positive this session is in comparison with the first. In fact, it led to a very good night's sleep and awakening the next day, although not totally free from all pain, in a very good frame of mind.

The reader should not think that these images will lead to instant relief – a complete remission. These are very rare. But session two does illustrate a positive attitude, an expectation of success. In addition, the feedback does allow you to feel that you are doing some good, and that further progress is possible. The next session was almost a Walt Disney cartoon.

Session 3   White cells once again attacked the remnants of a small bewildered cat (which was not even black any more). Then in came a team of little men. They washed down what appeared to be nerve fibres and set about doing a repair job. One amusing aspect was that they went about their work singing and playing (sliding down the nerve fibres). At one point a new section (like a piece of tubing) was inserted, while at another time a nerve ending (like a dendrite) was joined up to make contact.

This is a very positive scene with all indications that the body's repair mechanisms are at work, and 'allowed' to work. It is in this scene that a knowledge of the anatomy of nerves and the cause of the pain is useful.

The final session I intend to recount shows a change in the creature to be consulted. This is not illogical because the black cat has been eliminated. Earlier scenes tend to be acting on the spine in the middle portion of the back. However, the main source of trouble seems to be at the base. This is brought out in this final sequence. When asked to picture the pain there was a tightly clenched fist squeezing the nerves. When asked to form a creature, a man appeared – but almost wholly dominated by this clenched fist. He was not vicious, but rather seemed protective.

> *Session 4*   I asked him what he was doing and he replied that he was pulling the nerves away from a protruding bone. When I asked for it to be corrected, in came a group of men. One was deep in thought and considered it to be a hefty job. Brought in ropes and pullies. Rigged up and began to wind a reel which moved the bone. Ointment was then rubbed onto the bone and the man cautiously released the nerves. I asked if any more could be done. A foreman went and looked over the job and said not at the moment, 'You could warm it up, however'. Then in came a man with a blow lamp and began to brush the flame over the affected area. I then got him to switch off the flame so that I could awaken.

There is no doubt about the imagery in these scenes. The obvious concentration on repair is very important. The whole point about this approach to pain (or any illness) is to marshal the body's own defences and to get them to work for your own benefit. The question and answer sessions will lead to invaluable information about the cause of the problem and how you may overcome it. Even the final scene with the blow lamp is therapeutic because this is a simple image to raise the temperature of the surrounding area. Body temperature is controlled by the autonomic nervous system, but such imagery can bring it under conscious control. By raising the temperature there is an increase in blood flow to the affected area, and so more chance of healing. The imagery is shown here to help in the recovery programme.

One final observation: before you awaken you should picture yourself totally free from pain and doing all the things you want to do. You must see in your mind's eye the desired outcome and not simply your present state of health. This is not a question of self-deception. The subconscious mind works on different principles, as we discussed in Part I. By seeing the end result the mind carries out programmes for achieving those ends. Thus a programme of self-direction is initiated, and not one of self-deception.

Helping Your Own Healing Processes

Let us now turn to healing. We shall state the steps in brief first and then go on to discuss them in detail. The aim is to visualize the illness, the cure taking place and a healthy final outcome.

Procedure

Step 1   Get into a relaxed state as explained on page 10.

Step 2   Visualize your illness in whatever form appropriate to you. If necessary view it on a TV screen. You must attempt to visualize it with all of your senses.

Step 3   Picture the cure taking place as vividly as you can. Do not be afraid of making it bizarre. Incorporate in the image both the body's own healing mechanisms (e.g. white blood cells) and the medication you may be receiving from the doctor.

Step 4   Clean away all debris and unwanted waste. Picture the site being cleared and left free from illness.

Step 5   Picture yourself being free of the illness and performing a normal active life, also see yourself happy and healthy.

Step 6   Congratulate or thank yourself (i.e. your sub-conscious) for aiding in the cure.

Step 7   Wake yourself up.

This process should be repeated frequently. The more serious the illness the more frequently this should be done. It is especially useful if you are laid up in bed. If not, a few times will not go amiss. At night before going to sleep is a very good time, because you will bring your dreams to bear in the healing process as a consequence.

Now let me comment in more detail about some of the steps. Step 2 on visualizing your illness can be troublesome if you know nothing about it. Learn something about your illness or that part of the body involved. This does not have to be too detailed, but an odd sketch by the physician will aid here. Take hardening of the arteries, for instance, which can lead to high blood pressure and angina. This arises from fat deposits in the artery and to a blood clot in a constricted area, as shown in Figure 10. By having such a sketch to visualize, step 3 becomes a little easier.

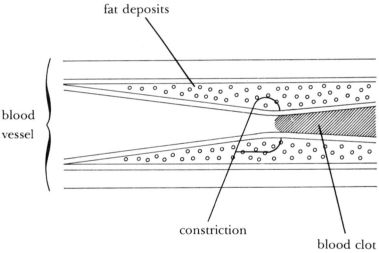

Figure 10

It may be that you can visualize your illness – bizarre as the picture may be. Then do so, because this will be thrown up by your own psyche. Sketch it after the session. This will allow you to see how your subconscious mind is 'seeing' the illness over a period of time. Comparing the sketches can be very rewarding.

The colour and texture of your illness can be very revealing also. Even sounds are possible (as in the case of the cat reported in the previous section). Colour is highly significant to the subconscious mind. It may be possible when trying step 3 to change the colour as a means of achieving a cure. Take special note of the colour of the offending party and the colour of your body's defences if these are in the scene. Also notice the colour, shape and texture of any medicine that you may be taking, if this too is in the scene.

The most ingenious and imaginative step is step 3. In this the aim is to picture a cure, the more bizarre probably the better. The symbolism is more important than whether it is realistic or not; so here the aim is to keep the idea of the goal uppermost. The goal is a complete cure.

To begin, take the hardening of the arteries as an example. It is best to create a scene in stages. From Figure 10 we notice three major problems:

1 Fat deposits
2 Blood clot
3 A constriction

Take each of these in turn. Imagine, say, a workforce and a man with a blow lamp coming in and melting the fat deposits. Picture this vividly and see the fat melting. Next see a group of men with shovels coming and digging out the blood clot, leaving the centre of the vessel free. Finally, have men come in and press out the lining of the blood vessel so that it is straight and wide. You can then go immediately into step 4 (or combine steps 3 and 4) and have cleaners come in and get rid of the waste, brushing it away and washing it all clean. See the vessel sparkling clean and ready for blood to come gushing down without any obstruction. See the blood coursing through. Thank the men for their good work (a part of step 6). At all times *see* and *feel* that an excellent job(s) is being done.

Step 5 is then to switch on your TV screen – explained fully in a later section. See yourself with no high blood pressure and free from any symptoms. Not only see yourself, but feel the health in the image and feel the emotion of joy at being healthy. It is most important that you *see* and *feel* the desired outcome on each occasion. Believe it will be so.

It is important to carry out step 6 of self-congratulation. In doing this you are talking to your inner self. If a doctor cured you then you would thank him. So why not your inner self? Is he/she no less important? Your self-image needs encouragement to work in your favour, and step 6 helps in achieving this. It also has the effect of creating a positive self-assured image of your inner self, a confidence and assuredness which is very beneficial as well as being therapeutic.

Pointers in Forming Images
Image formation is not a passive act and you must work at creating vivid and useful images. Knowing something about the anatomy and physiology of your particular area of pain or illness can help in forming images.

Clearly you will only feel pain if a message is sent up

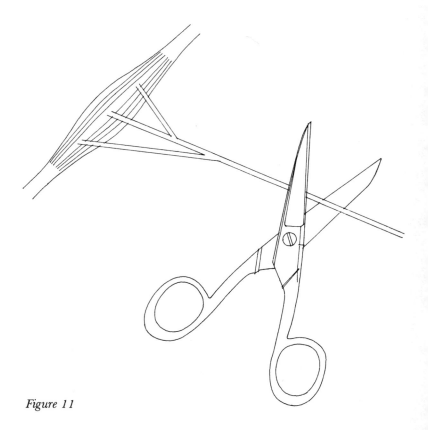

Figure 11

through the nerves to the brain. How can you prevent such a message being sent? Simply cut the nerve – in your mind's eye of course! Suppose you have a pain or ache in some muscle. You can imagine a scene like that in Figure 11.

It is important that the scissors are big and sharp so that they can carry out their task. An alternative image is given in Figure 12, where we have imagined fish swallowing the chemical which transmits the electrical impulse from one neuron to the next. Both images have the same objective – to prevent the message from travelling up to the brain.

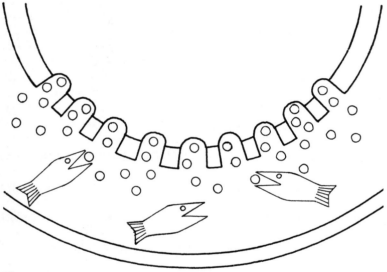

Figure 12

We can get a guide on image formation by considering what aspirin does. Aspirin carries out three functions:

1   It relieves pain
2   It lowers temperature
3   It reduces inflammation

It is a medication for headache and bone and muscle pain – but not for intense pain or pain associated with internal organs. In relieving pain it probably reduces the transmission of nerve impulses. This we have just dealt with. In dealing with inflammation some picture involving the affected area being bathed will help. Have a fireman with a hose wash away all the dead or inflamed cells, so leaving the area free of injury. If you are already taking some prescribed medicine you can incorporate this into the scene. You can imagine the medicine as globules or some form of creature coming in and attacking the inflammation. But once again, have the site cleared of all debris so as to leave the area free from all damage.

The body has its own army for defence and these are the white blood cells. It is always useful to incorporate these in your healing images. Visualize them as an army, a vast formidable army. If you are having any negative thoughts or feelings your army will be small and puny and not up to the task. You must picture an invincible army. If you are taking medicine have the army divided into foot soldiers (the white blood cells) and the artillery (the medication). Picture both achieving their individual successes. When the battle is over and won (naturally!) see the battlefield being cleaned up. In other words, picture your body getting rid of all its waste and toxic substances. If necessary think of a water system with the waste being piped away (to the kidneys, in fact) and then flushed out.

The images can be very bizarre, so long as they indicate the desired result. They can involve mythical creatures, goblins or things from outer space. The aim, however, is to achieve belief in the efficacy of the image. Many will spring into awareness purely on their own and these should be utilized and embellished upon. If they are in colour enhance the vividness of the colours even more. One possibility is to picture the pain or illness, in whatever form, then project it out of the body as if it were in space and you were looking at it. Then change its shape and colour. Distort it by your will. If you can do this, then make it very small and change its colour to one 'milder' and put the pain or illness back. Keep doing this on repeated occasions until the problem is projected and disappears, i.e. until there is nothing to project back into your body.

Two final observations are worth making. First, you should congratulate yourself on your co-operation, just as you would if you got help from another person. Family and friends tend, over time, to be taken for granted. This is even more true of our own subconscious mind. It is not clear why this act of congratulation works, but it is important and you should do it on every occasion. Second, it is not being suggested here that you should ignore all pain or illness. Both are a signalling device which tells you something is wrong. But sometimes the pain or illness is unnecessary and is giving a signal more for your emotional well-being. In the case of toothache, for instance, you know the pain is telling you to see a dentist. But until that time any alleviation of the pain will be of help.

Using a TV Screen

Television has undoubtedly become an integral part of our society, for good and bad. One survey across twelve countries indicates that of an average working day men spend almost 7 per cent of their time involved in the mass media leisure pursuits, while for women it is under 5 per cent. Considering work accounts for 40 per cent and 33 per cent respectively, this is a high percentage. The greatest element of this is spent watching TV. Over a lifetime quite a considerable amount of time is spent watching TV. Having stated the obvious, it is important to realize that we can utilize this conditioning – for that is what it is! If you want a child to visualize something you can do no better than suggest that he or she close their eyes and see a TV set. Then have them imagine it being switched on and seeing their favourite show. Their change in facial expression is enough to indicate their willingness and ability to do this. They also enjoy carrying out this 'game'.

The same idea can be utilized by older people – and many who find visualization difficult have greater success with this technique. As part of the steps listed on page 141, it is assumed that you already have your eyes closed. The object is to visualize a large TV screen which initially is switched off. First you outline what you will see when you switch on the screen. For instance, you may say to yourself that when you switch on the TV you are going to see the inside of your ear, stomach or whatever. This is where a knowledge of your problem can help. Find pictures of whatever difficulty you have so that you can form some image on the screen. If you find this difficult, imagine seeing an operating theatre with doctors surrounding a patient – you. See and hear them discuss the problem and the fact that they can cure it. The basic object at this point is to be able to visualize your problem in some way or other. Suggest *hearing* it, *feeling* it and *seeing* it – colours and all.

Now have the set switched on. Two possibilities can occur at this point. Either you 'see' nothing or you 'see' something. If you see something then again two possibilities arise. Either you see something close to what you suggested you would see, or you find that your imagination throws up a totally different image of its own choosing. If you see nothing then you must keep trying. If you see what has been suggested then fine. If your imagination throws onto the screen some bizarre scene which contains your problem then accept this readily. For instance, if some problem has arisen because of a car crash then such a scene may readily come on the set. At this stage the important thing is to get some image of your problem on the set.

Now have the scene change. One possibility is to see the picture move off from the left to the right – but this is not essential. What is necessary is that you are able to replace one scene by another very readily. If necessary switch channels! The new scene is one that you are going to work on; one in which you are going to see, hear and feel some drama unfold which eliminates, or reduces, whatever problem you are working on. You can make this as vivid and as fantastic as you like and can continue the image for as long as you like. The object, however, is to produce a series of interrelated images which have as their final outcome a fully healthy and cured person. This final stage is very important. You are not engaging in wishful thinking, but rather in *goal-directed imagery*. You are visualizing what you would like to be and so creating healing forces in you to achieve that goal. The goal is what initiates the forces of change and correction. To repeat, you are not engaging in wishful thinking, but rather in goal-directed imagery. For the success of goal-directed imagery in dealing with health, you must:

– *desire* a cure
– *believe* a cure is possible
– *expect* a cure

A positive attitude must involve all three elements: desire, belief and expectancy.

An Inner-Body Search

One difficulty encountered in a number of illnesses is knowing *where* in the body the problem lay. Pain, say, in the shoulder does not necessarily mean that it is the shoulder which is the source of the problem. Pain tends to be referred, i.e. passed over to a different locality from its source. A classic example of this is migraine. It is possible to use creative visualization to explore the inside of the body and find the source of a problem.

To undertake this search does not require you to know human anatomy and physiology, but a rough idea of the blood system, the digestive system and the endocrine glands would aid considerably. You could simply let the search 'take its own course'. Your subconscious mind has access to vast knowledge built into your genetic code – far superior knowledge than we are presently aware of (i.e. consciously aware of). In letting the search 'take its own course' this knowledge can be subconsciously utilized.

The idea is quite straightforward to describe, but requires some working at to be used proficiently. Basically, the aim is to enter your body, search around and finally come out!

First, get into a relaxed state as explained on page 10. To enter your body you must change yourself: you must become very small. Visualize yourself shrinking in size. Anyone who has read or seen the film version of Isaac Asimov's *Fantastic Voyage* will immediately see what is to happen. In this film a famous person has a brain tumour which can only be eliminated by 'internal brain surgery'. A group of people are shrunk in size then added to a liquid (they themselves are in a sort of space vessel) and injected into the blood-stream. They make their way through the body and clear the tumour with a laser and finally make their exit through the tear-duct in the eye. Quite a fantastic voyage indeed. The same is being suggested here.

Once you are very small you can visualize yourself entering your body. In the film just recounted this was directly into the blood-stream. Another way may be to crawl up through the nostril, or down the throat, or even through a sweat gland. It does not really matter how, so long as entry into the body is achieved.

Once in your body you can take a look around. See the linings on the walls and observe the various parts of the body. It is here that a knowledge of the blood system and nervous system will help. You can imagine using the blood-stream as a means of travel. Imagine getting into your own underwater vessel – which has a large domed window at the front so that you can see everything (a sort of Nautilus of your own). On the first occasion ignore your problem and simply get used to the idea of exploring inside your body. Once you have experienced an inside exploration you can direct your search to your specific problem.

When you have finished exploring, come out of your body in a similar fashion to the way you went in. Then see yourself return to normal size.

This is not an easy exercise but it can be a very rewarding one. Like all experiences, it becomes easier with practice. When seeking out your problem take note of what it looks like, its colour and size; also how you feel about it. All these may help on subsequent occasions.

Conclusion

What I have attempted to show in this chapter is how the mind and body can be made to relate to one another for the benefit of the individual. The mind and body are interlinked in a very complex way. To assume all illness is a body malfunction is simply wrong. To assume it is all in the mind is equally wrong. The truth, as more people are coming to see 'truth', is that illness arises from an imbalance between the mind and the body. When this imbalance occurs a person becomes vulnerable to pain, infections, accidents, etc. The infection, say, has undoubted body manifestations. To say the illness is therefore somatic is naive. What plays a part, but only a part, is why the person was vulnerable to such an infection. Holistic medicine tries to deal with the whole person – mind and body. Until such time as we understand these issues better, the individual is left to his or her own devices in re-uniting mind and body. Present-day medicine considers that the individual is superfluous in bringing about his or her own cure: give the patient the right tablet or injection and all will be well. Not so. Many people – not least doctors – have come to realize that this is far from the complete answer. The individual can contribute to his or her own cure. The basic problem is knowing how, and this chapter is a brief attempt to show you how by means of creative visualization.

11
OTHER USES

In this brief final chapter the aim is two-fold. First, to supply a creative visualization which raises your general energy level and is very good for periods of depression – a visualization the author has found most effective. Second, to wet the appetite by suggesting a number of other areas where creative visualization can be applied.

Raising Your Energy Level

Work during the day depletes our energy. Some days seem more draining than others, and some begin with a low stock of energy because of a poor night's sleep. One reason why we rest and sleep is so that we can restore the body's energy. The relaxation periods where you engage in creative visualization will naturally raise your body's energy level. You can, however, use a specific visualization to achieve this.

The one about to be presented came to me during a relaxation period which I was undertaking after a period when I was feeling fairly drained from working hard and I wanted a visualization that would replenish my energy. I was quite surprised at how effective it was and have suggested it to other people, who have also found it very effective. There are few words in this creative visualization and it is largely creating a very vivid scene. But let me take you through it step by step.

Raising the body's energy

While in a relaxed state you imagine yourself lying on a bed with your eyes closed. A beam of sunlight comes down from the sun and envelopes your whole body. You then rise up and pass up the beam of sunlight into the heart of the sun. (At this stage you imagine yourself naked.) When you reach the heart of the sun you open up your arms and legs making an X shape, including opening up your hands and fingers. You then simply imagine that you are absorbing into your body health-giving energy. Really *feel* the energy going into your body. (Your body may very well tingle during this creative visualization.) If you like, you can at this point add a series of suggestions. They can go something like this . . .

I can feel the energy from the sun passing into my body. Yes, my body is drawing energy from the sun—energy that my body needs, energy that will revitalize all my body, energy that will pass into every cell and every organ of my body. (Keep this up until you feel that your body has sufficient energy – a feeling which is not too difficult to recognize.)

When you feel fully energized, bring your arms and legs together, pass back down the sunbeam and return to your lying position on the bed.

This particular visualization can be engaged in either at the end of a session or simply when you feel depleted of energy. It is very good if you are feeling depressed, because depression creates a low level of body energy and the present creative visualization can reverse the process.

Other Uses

Creative visualization can be used to get more achievement and/or more fulfilment out of any job or hobby. Chapter 5 on *Imagery in Business Situations* illustrated just some uses in the work context. But it does not matter what job you have, creative visualization can be employed. It can be used to give you a different perspective about the job; e.g. changing your attitude if you formerly found it depressing and unrewarding a feature of your negative thinking and not necessarily the job). It can be used to improve your efficiency and it can be used in arriving at new ideas which can help in your job.

When our jobs are rather mundane, however, no amount of creative visualization can make them less so. In this situation relationships can be improved, as outlined in Chapter 5. But often people with such jobs find that they require hobbies of a creative nature to balance the mundaneness of their job. It may be music, art, flower arranging, gardening or computer programming. It is in these areas that creative visualization can be used to great effect. Simply use the ideas given throughout this book and adapt them to your own particular hobby. Your hobby will then take on a new lease of life and become even more creative and more satisfying.

FURTHER READING

Assagioli, R., *Psychosynthesis* (Turnstone Press, 1965).
Assagioli, R., *The Act of Will* (Wildwood House, 1973).
Asimov, I., *Fantastic Voyage* (Granada, 1966).
Buzan, T., *Use Your Head* (BBC Publications, 1974).
Buzan, T., *Make The Most of Your Mind* (Pan, 1977).
Capra, F., *The Tao of Physics* (Fontana, 1975).
Dineen, J., *Remembering Made Easy* (Thorsons, 1977).
Faraday, A., *Dream Power* (Pan, 1972).
Faraday, A., *The Dream Game* (Penguin, 1974).
Ferrucci, P., *What We May Be* (Turnstone Press, 1982).
French, J. D., *The Reticular Formation* in *Scientific America* (1957).
Gallwey, W. T., *The Inner Game of Tennis* (Random House, 1974).
Gallwey, W. T., with Kriegal, B., *Inner Skiing* (Random House, 1977).
Gallwey, W. T., *The Inner Game of Golf* (Jonathan Cape, 1981).
Garfield, P., *Creative Dreaming* (Futura, 1974).
Hall, C. S., *What People Dream About* in *Scientific America* (1951).
Harding, D. E., *On Having No Head* in D. R. Hofstadter and D. C. Dennet *The Mind's I* (Penguin, 1981).
Hofstadter, D. R. and Dennet, D. C., *The Mind's I* (Penguin, 1981).
Hunt, M. *The Universe Within* (Harvester Press, 1982).
Kafka, F., *Metamorphosis*. (First published 1916). (Penguin, 1961).
Lorayne, H., *How to Develop a Super-Power Memory* (A Thomas and Company, 1958).
Lowen, A., *Bioenergetics* (Penguin, 1975).
McKeller, P., *Experience and Behaviour* (Penguin, 1968).
Ophiel, *The Art and Practice of Getting Material Things Through Creative Visualization* (Thorsons, 1967).

Ouspensky, P. D. *In Search of the Miraculous* (Routledge & Kegan Paul, 1950).

Ouspensky, P. D., *The Fourth Way* (Routledge & Kegan Paul, 1957).

Pearls, F. S., Hefferline, R. F., and Goodman, P., *Gestalt Therapy* (Penguin, 1951).

Rosa, K., *Autogenic Training* (Victor Gollancz, 1976).

Russel, P., *The Brain Book* (Routledge & Kegan Paul, 1979).

Shone, R., *Autohypnosis* (Thorsons, 1982).

Simonton, O. C., *et al*, *Getting Well Again* (Bantam Books, 1978).

Singer, J. L., *Daydreaming and Fantasy* (Oxford University Press, 1976).

Wright, D. S. *et al*, *Introducing Psychology* (Penguin, 1970).

Young, J. Z., *Programs of the Brain* (Oxford University Press, 1978).

Zimbardo, P. G., *Shyness* (Pan, 1977).

INDEX